FAMILY COMMUNICATION

AN INTEGRATED SYSTEMS APPROACH

Evelyn Sieburg, Ph.D.

GARDNER PRESS, INC.

New York   London

GARDNER PRESS, INC.
19 Union Square West
New York 10003

Library of Congress Cataloging-in-Publication Data

Sieburg, Evelyn.
   Family communication.

   Bibliography: p.
   Includes index.
   1. Family. 2. Communication in marriage. 3. Parent
and child. 4. Problem family—Counseling of. I. Title.
HQ734.S593 1985   306.8′5   85-13203
ISBN 0-89876-109-3

Book Design by Publishers Creative Services

Printed in the United States of America

Contents

FAMILY
COMMUNICATION

AN
INTEGRATED
SYSTEMS
APPROACH

Preface

This book is about how people in families talk, act, and relate with one another. In writing it, I have drawn freely from many disciplines—sociology, linguistics, clinical psychology, family psychiatry, general system theory, general semantics, ego psychology, communication theory, and others. The value of the work lies in my drawing together for the non-professional reader selected findings and insights from these various sources.

Originally I had no thought of producing a creative synthesis—only to present in one easy-to-read volume an overview of the writings and theoretical views that seemed to have relevance for the study of family communication. As the data-gathering progressed, I began to see notable areas of substantive agreement among scholars with very different orientations, leading me to the exciting suspicion that what goes on among family members is fully rule-governed and potentially predictable. What was to have been a simple recounting of various "functional" and "dysfunctional" communicative patterns in families began to fall, almost on its own, into quite different groupings. These eventually suggested a more elaborate typology of family systems according to style of response, but one that also reflected systemic features and relational characteristics. The material, representing the culmination of a lengthy literature review extending over many years, is presented in summary form in Table 14.1 at the end of Part V. It may be that this will provide a starting place for those who will eventually synthesize and formalize the study of family communication.

I undertook to write this book because, in my own experience teaching family communication courses to undergraduate and graduate students and conducting family communication seminars and workshops for people of varying educational levels, I have been dissatisfied with the material available for outside reading. Some of the most insightful theories, exciting research breakthroughs, and conceptual innovations about family interaction cannot usually be assigned to students, simply because the level of writing makes them incomprehensible except to other professionals in the field. Sociologists frequently write for other sociologists; ego psychologists write for an audience already well-grounded in psychoanalytic theory and familiar with its terminology; experimental psychologists are quite inscrutable to the reader untrained in statistical procedures. Because I believe that many of these scholars have things to say that are potentially valuable to a general audience, I have undertaken to "translate" some of the more important views and findings into simpler language.

Although the family is, in some respects, a unique gathering, it is, in other respects, not unique at all. In addition to its quality of "family-ness," it is also a group, system, a communication network, and a tapestry of interdependent, interpersonal relationships. One achieves a broad understanding of family interaction by becoming aware of the family's many aspects. For this reason, I have drawn from sources not customarily thought of as relevant to the family: small group theory, general system theory, and interpersonal theory.

It is necessary for any piece of writing to have a conceptual framework, even when the writer is looking at the same basic material from different points of view, and this book—despite its wide-ranging sources—is no exception. Human communication is my special field, so I have tried to deal with communication variables rather than with sociological, economic, or biological variables. I have, therefore, omitted many interesting ideas that are only indirectly related to family communication. For instance, I have not dealt with family problems arising out of in-law interference, budget mishandling, alcohol abuse, or child battering. Certainly families at times talk *about* these serious matters at great length, but it seems to me that the focus of this book dictated the study of communication *process* rather than content.

Wherever possible, I have stayed with the notion of the family as a system—a dynamic whole composed of constantly shifting interrelationships, but still bounded, and rule-governed. This does not mean that the discussions in this book are always limited to the systems properties of families; indeed, this kind of literature is very sparse. There are places where it seemed appropriate to comment on the individual traits of a member as though these were sufficiently explanatory, or to cite research based on the observation of dyads or triads within the family group. Ideally, I believe, family research methods should include all three levels: individual properties, dyadic properties (husband-wife, mother-child, father-child, and child-child), as well as system properties. Unfortunately, this multi-level type of family research is still in its infancy, although, as Broderick noted in 1971, general system theory offers a base for such integration.

The family as a subject of scientific investigation has been approached over the years (since approximately the mid-nineteenth century) from many different directions, representing a variety of disciplines, theoretical orientations, and conceptual viewpoints. It is not my purpose here to attempt a review of the history of family research and theory, but only to take note of the complexity and range of such research and to acknowledge some of its problems and challenges.

Virtually all the social and behavioral sciences have addressed the "family" and family interaction. What each scholar chooses to study, however, is somewhat dictated by his or her particular field of study. The sociologist usually sees family communication as a manifestation of roles, social influence, dominance, and other structural features common to all social systems. The social psychologist or group theorist who studies the family may be interested in the same things as the sociologist, but extends the study of families to include such formulations as conformity, cohesiveness, satisfaction, interaction nets, and leadership styles. The clinical researcher tends to focus on "unhealthy" forms of family interaction and seeks better ways of measuring therapeutic change. The communication scholar may adopt any or all of the foregoing conceptualizations but is primarily concerned with messages and their transmission, including such elements as language, semantics, feedback, and information processing.

Within the scope of his or her own discipline, each researcher also selects a conceptual framework as a basis for further study. In 1960 Reuben Hill and D.A. Hansen identified five such frameworks for family research, labeling them Institutional, Structural-Functional, Symbolic Interactional, Situational, and Developmental. Although this classification exerted much influence on family research during the decade of the 1960s, it has largely given way to various newer and more theoretically specific models, such as balance theory, game theory, and—most relevant to this book—general system theory, a model which, in the opinion of Carlfred B. Broderick, "deserves a great deal more notice than it has received" (*Journal of Marriage and the Family*, Feb. 1971, p. 144).

Significantly, Broderick did not suggest that general system theory (GST) is, in itself, sufficient to explain all observed family interaction, or even that it is superior to other orientations. What he did say is that GST is "able to accommodate all that is viable in other frameworks also." In other words, general system theory can conceivably be used as a research base for integrating other models, and even other disciplines, when relevant. This is the viewpoint I have taken throughout the book. Although it is far from being the true integration Broderick envisioned, it makes use of data derived from many different models without losing sight of the original conceptualization of the family as a system.

Much of the material used here comes from clinical

sources, because, probably more than any other field, family psychiatry and family psychotherapy are concerned with whole-family problems. This has the disadvantage of over-representing troubled families and neglecting "normal" ones. It is perhaps inevitable that this is so, because, as Broderick commented, "concern with family organization seems most often to be a spin-off of concern for family *dis*organization." Because there has been greater motivation for researchers to study troubled families, they have been given more attention and closer scrutiny; hence, more information is available about them than about untroubled families. The seeming emphasis on family pathology throughout this book should not obscure the fact that many families are healthy and viable systems that support satisfying relationships, authentic interaction, and confirming styles of response.

Three clinical research groups that studied schizophrenic communication in families have contributed enormously to the understanding of pathological family systems, and I have used their work extensively: (1) the Bateson group in Palo Alto, which started out to study the paradoxes of abstraction in communication and eventually developed the double-bind hypothesis of schizophrenia, a formulation directly relevant to family communication; (2) the Lidz group at Yale University, which took a rather orthodox psychoanalytic view of families but contributed to a systems approach by identifying whole families as "skewed" (centered around a single strong, do-minant, parental figure, while the other parent remained weak and withdrawn), or those families in which the marital couple lived in a state of "schism" (where relations are characterized by chronic hostility and mutual withdrawal); (3) the Wynne group at the National Institute of Mental Health in Bethesda, Maryland, whose focus was more related to traditional in-dividual psychology than to a systems approach, but which nevertheless added significantly to the total-family concep-tualization with their description of family "mutuality" and "pseudomutuality." The work of these groups is discussed in Part III.

Methods of collecting and interpreting data about the family are even more varied than are the underlying theories. All empirical research, of course, requires observations of some sort, but the observational scheme selected and the kind of data collected ranges widely. Some researchers observe a family in its natural home environment while others insist that a laboratory setting permits better control of variables. Some researchers stimulate family discussions with the use of group tasks or questionnaires; others let the family interact naturally without structure. Some observe a single family and report on it as a case study; other research strategies require the comparison of one kind of family with another (as "disturbed" vs. "normal," or "clinical" vs. "non-clinical"). Still others count certain interaction or outcome features (how many times did the family do that in the course of the observation?), such as recurring themes, "process" events, nonverbal behaviors, emotional events, or interactional patterns. An abundance of rating scales and instruments are available to aid the researcher in recording whatever aspect of family interaction he or she chooses to observe.

In addition to questions of conceptualization, theory base, and method, the family researcher faces some very practical difficulties in studying whole-family interaction. Some of the most frequently voiced complaints are:

(1) Families are reluctant to be observed or to have their interaction analyzed. Since it is considered unethical to observe a family without its knowledge and permission, the result is that researchers are prone to use the families of acquaintances and friends, or members of some particular group, such as church members or co-workers. This weakens the conclusions that can be drawn, because, without random selection, there is no assurance that the findings can be generalized beyond the group observed.

(2) Even when families are willing to be observed for research purposes, they do not necessarily behave in the same way that they would under natural (un-observed) conditions. This may reflect a simple self-consciousness about "acting right" for the benefit of an observer; or it may be evidence of the transactional principle discussed in Chapter 1, that the addition or deletion of a component changes the entire system; the family with a new member in the form of an observer is not the "same" system as it was before the addition. Whatever the explanation, this phenomenon occurs

in most observational research of families and appears unavoidable.

(3) A related problem is that of getting whole families together at the same time to interact for a researcher. The complexities of arranging for extended periods of observed interaction of a family with a working father (and probably a working mother as well), several children in school at different hours, various social commitments, and/or a member who does not live at home full-time (but still influences the family's behavior)—all tempt a researcher to take whatever he or she can get and to generalize, perhaps unjustifiably, about how the family-as-a-whole interacts when all together.

(4) It is easier and less costly to do research based on linear models than to attempt system-based research. To begin with, systems research requires new tools and designs not generally familiar to the family researcher. Even with trained researchers, systems-based research requires the collection of large amounts of data usually over long periods of time. Although the use of computer applications has helped, the effort is often prohibitively expensive and time-consuming. Even in the face of such handicaps, however, the need for continued work at a systemic level is recognized in order to arrive at a better understanding of the total family.

The plan of this book is to present several perspectives of the family: as it appears from a general system view, as a communication system, as a relational system, and as an interactional response system. The various aspects are clearly interrelated and seem fully consistent with one another, although each has a somewhat different focus and uses a different nomenclature. My goal has been to present these various points of view in a way that is understandable to students; and to suggest how a family's interaction patterns of response are reflected in its systems properties, its communicative properties, and in its relational properties. There are ample grounds, it appears, for believing that we are all talking about the same things. For example, a family that is described in system terms as having "impermeable external boundaries" can also be described in interactional terms as having an "impervious" style of response that is heavy on denial and distortion. By the same token, a family with "weak interconnections" is likely to interact in a way that is identified as "indifferent."

I have tried to keep technical language out of the book. Where it has been unavoidable, as in the discussion of general system theory, I have immediately explained the terms as simply as possible. To discuss family behavior with such words as "homeostasis" or "equifinality," however, in no way denies that we are looking at how real people in real families live their lives together.

This book is an attempt to create linkages among the various views of a family. The five parts of the book examine the various aspects of the family. The final chapter considers how the preceding views might be synthesized by describing four theoretical family types according to each type's system properties, relational styles, characteristic-message form and flow, associated pathologies, and response styles.

It is not possible to be completely objective about family interaction; even the process of selecting certain material for inclusion reflects my subjective bias. Nevertheless, although this is not an *advice* book, nor intended as a guide for better parenting or as a marriage manual, the reader cannot fail to get the message that straight talk is better than sham, that individual autonomy is better than family merger—is, in fact, essential for loving relationships, that open systems are preferable to the rigid orthodoxy of closed systems. Like all persons who hold biases, I am convinced that my own have substantial support from the experts and are well-grounded in fact, however weak the research upon which such "facts" are based.

My hope is that this book will generate in the reader an excitement and curiosity about the burgeoning field of family communication. Perhaps it will cause the reader to notice things about his or her own family's interaction that were not noticed before, to appreciate aspects of family relating previously taken for granted. Perhaps the reader might even become a bit more skeptical about the values of a society that is not noted for its healthy family communication.

A list of references follows each of the five sections of the book.

Acknowledgments

To start at the beginning, I want to thank Dr. Alvin Goldberg, Dr. Alton Barbour, and Dr. Carl Larson of the University of Denver's Speech Communication Department for their help and encouragement in my early struggles to conceptualize and measure interpersonal confirmation and disconfirmation. Their support was important even before the book was conceived of. My thanks also to Dr. Judy Goldberg for her enthusiasm about the writing of a family communication book in the first place, and for her collaboration, in its earliest stages. My special appreciation to Dr. Kenneth Cissna at the University of South Florida, who has worked with me over the years in clarifying and refining the concept of interpersonal confirmation and in keeping track of research in the area. I am also indebted to special friends and colleagues for constructive critical reviews of the manuscript and helpful suggestions for its improvement: Ann Liem, who contributed her excellent editorial skills in early drafts of the manuscript; Dr. Vicki Weatherford of Solana Beach, California, whose suggestions have had a profound influence on the finished work; Mary Cell of La Jolla, California, and Dr. Patricia O'Halloran of San Diego, who, because of their expertise as practicing family therapists, were able to add important practical touches to the final draft. I also wish to express special appreciation to philosopher Maurice Friedman, Professor of Religious Studies, Philosophy, and Comparative Literature at San Diego State University, and recognized authority in the writings of Martin Buber, for his review of the chapters (12 and 13) about confirmation and his suggestions for improvement. I am indebted to them all.

PART I

THE FAMILY AS SYSTEM

CHAPTER 1

The Nature of Systems:
Background and Principles

A family is made up of individual people, yet we can never fully understand its behavior by examining its members one at a time. This would be much like trying to understand an automobile by looking at each of its disassembled parts. We could learn some things about the car but would miss the most important aspect of all—how the parts work together to form a functioning whole, how each part affects the other parts, and what each contributes to the total operation.

The notion that a "whole" can be understood only by studying its parts *in relation to each other* and *in relation to the total operation* suggests von Bertalanffy's definition of a system as a "complex of interacting elements" (Bertalanffy, 1968, p. 19). An even simpler explanation is that by Beer, who says, "anything that consists of parts connected together will be called a system" (Beer, 1964, p. 9). Either definition is broad enough to include solar systems, chemical formulas, changes in natural ecology, and fluctuations of the stock market. It is also a good way to begin in the study of family communication.

An immediate difficulty in identifying any given system is that the observer cannot always tell at a glance which parts are interacting to form a whole, nor can the observer see the precise nature of the connections between parts. To illustrate the problem of determining the boundary of a system, Lederer and Jackson (1968) give the following account:

> ...in Canada an official in the wildlife study bureau observed that the rabbit population in one area had diminished considerably. Scientists tried to discover what illness had attacked the rabbits, but found none. A few years later the rabbit population increased; then later, again, it diminished. The scientists could find no illness, the reason for these cycles in the rabbit population remained a mystery. At approximately the same time, other officials in the wildlife bureau noticed population fluctuation among foxes. They too sought—and did not find— epidemics among the foxes which might explain these cycles.
>
> By chance, the reports about the varying rabbit population and the varying fox population got to the desk of the same scientist, and having both reports he soon solved the mystery. When the rabbit population increased, so did the fox population. When there were a great many rabbits, the foxes had plenty of food, so they multiplied. But when the large numbers of foxes ate the large numbers of rabbits, the rabbit population declined. Now there was not enough food to support a large fox population, and the number of foxes declined. (p. 88)

Although the boundaries of a family "system" are more readily apparent and the human components of a family more easily recognized as parts of a whole, we still often make a mistake much like that of the wildlife officials by assuming that we can study each member alone—his personality and propensities—and then understand the total family's behavior by combining the various personalities in some additive fashion. (It is even unlikely that we could understand each member individually if we studied him or her apart from the context, as a separate object in space.)

That systems are "non-summative"—that "the whole is more than the sum of its parts"—had been recognized by natural scientists long before social and behavioral scientists began to observe that the same general rule seemed to apply equally well to human groups. Chemists, for instance, knew that two substances, when combined, would sometimes be transformed into an entirely new product; astronomers knew that the movement of a planet was part of a total configuration of movements of bodies in a solar system; and biologists knew that some insecticides could change the ecological balance of an entire geographical area. A commonplace illustration can be found in any kitchen, where a cook knows that the cake that comes out of the oven is nothing like the flour, eggs, and milk that went into the mix. All these otherwise dissimilar events can be classified as *systems*, which means that they all can, at least in part, be explained according to the principles that apply to *all* systems. This chapter will briefly trace the development of scientific thinking about systems and their attributes. Chapter 2 will then consider how some of these same attributes may also apply to family systems.

FIELD THEORY

The notion of the family as a system has deep roots in the natural and physical sciences as well as in philosophy and sociology. Before the turn of the century sociologist Emile Durkheim declared that any human group can properly be regarded as a system, but this idea was slow in gaining acceptance, particularly among psychologists who continued to regard the human being as the appropriate unit of study, and who believed further that they could examine and treat the mind apart from the total being, *and* apart from that being's environment. The most significant contributions to systems theory as applied to human groups, however, was made by a psychologist, Kurt Lewin, who came to the United

States in 1933 as a refugee from Hitler's Germany. Underlying much of Lewin's work is a set of principles adopted from the natural sciences and identified as *field theory.*

Field theory did not originate with Lewin, but was part of a movement about that time that cut across many disciplines. It was, in a sense, a revolt against the earlier-held belief that it is possible to explain natural events as "simple forces acting between unalterable particles." Thus, it had previously been argued, if one knew all about each particle—its size, shape, velocity, direction of movement, and so on, then one could predict what would happen when that particle encountered other particles. This view had proved accurate in many instances, but technological advances in the twentieth century had produced some unexplained exceptions. In some studies evidence was growing that the "simple forces" were themselves changed by the force fields in which they existed or through which they passed. In other words, the behavior of a particle depended only partially on its own characteristics; it was also influenced by the state of the field, and the field, of course, included the presence of other particles.

By substituting "person" for "particle" in the last sentence it is easy to understand Lewin's proposition that human behavior (B) is a function (f) of life space (LS), which in turn is a product of the interaction between a person (P) and his/her environment (E). Lewin expressed this in the form of an equation: $B = f(LS) = f(P,E)$. Although in Lewin's model the individual is conceptualized as an enclosed figure surrounded on all sides by a continuous personal boundary, the enclosed figure is always shown within a larger boundary representing the life space, which includes all factors that have an effect on the individual's behavior at any given time (Lewin, 1951).

Lewin himself did not deal specifically with the family as a group, but his theorizing about groups in general raised serious doubts about views then held about the family. In addition, his ideas helped to revolutionize the practice of psychiatry which, until that time, insisted that the individual patient could best be treated *outside* his or her family. Following Lewin, many psychiatrists began to regard the whole family as the "patient," introducing the new field of family psychotherapy. Some specific models for treatment of family systems are discussed in Part IV.

Two of Kurt Lewin's formulations derived from gestalt psychology, are fundamental to the study of family systems: (1) *Parts and elements do not exist in isolation but are organized into wholes*, and (2) *Behavior is dynamic rather than mechanistic*. The first is a restatement of what we have already said about systems, but the second requires further explanation. If the whole is more than the sum of its parts, then it follows that the behavior of each part results not only from its own characteristics, but also from its relationships with other parts, and with the whole. It is the "mechanistic" view that if a whole could be separated into its component parts and then reassembled into a different arrangement, each part would still perform its original function—in fact, would be incapable of performing any other function. Although this may be true of a mechanical system such as an automobile engine (a carburetor can only "carburate"), it is not true of a human component, which has a wide range of possible behaviors from which to select, depending upon the state of its relations and interconnections with other components (persons) at any given time. This principle has the effect of denying a static, one-way causality in favor of a view that describes elements in a constant state of interaction and change. It also means than any human system's parts, if rearranged in relation to other parts, will behave *differently* than they did before because they are not the "same" parts as before. Additionally, this principle means that the adding or deleting of parts will change the functioning of each remaining part and, of course, will change the functioning of the system.

In a way, the dynamic attribute of Lewin's field theory simply provides a theoretical explanation for something that most people recognize from their own experience: a persons' behavior is not uniformly the same in all circumstances, but changes with different people and different circumstances.

TRANSACTIONALISM

Somewhat paralleling Lewin's scientific approach to the study of human groups was the development of a philosophical concept known as transactionalism, or sometimes called *the transactional perspective.* This is essentially a restatement of Hegel's eighteenth-century dialectic principle, but has been expressed most clearly in modern times by John Dewey and A. F. Bentley in their classic book *Knowing and the Known* (1949). In this work, the authors described three ways of explaining any happening: (1) things act under their own powers, (2) there is a direct causal connection between a single stimulus and a single response where "thing is balanced against thing in causal interconnectedness", and (3) one observes the full system without attributing any cause to any single element in the system (transactionalism).

The first view [self-action] supposes than an examination of the components will reveal the source [or cause] of the system's behavior, while transactionalism assumes that examination of the components will reveal no more than each component as it is in itself, and will show nothing of how the component behaves in relation to other components. *The second view* supposes that a causal relationship exists between components and that the relationship is "linear"; that is, a single observed action has a single cause. The third view, transactionalism, assumes that the state of the system at any given time is the only true "effect." Thus, the observed behavior of any component is as attributable to the *effected* component as it is to the *causal* component.

Although transactionalism can be applied to all sorts of events, it is especially appropriate for the study of human communication, which, as Birdwhistell commented, "is not to be understood as a simple model of action and reaction, however complexly stated. As a system, it is to be comprehended on the transactional level" (1959, p. 104). Nevertheless, the average person tends to think of his or her family's behavior in terms of simple cause-effect, stimulus-response. One member is seen as active, and the other, as passive; one acts and the other reacts. This sort of thinking is so commonly accepted in our culture than in the opening sessions of marriage or family counseling, the entire time may be taken up with charges and counter-charges, in an almost desperate attempt to establish blame and make it clear to the counselor who it was that "started" the problems that brought the family members to therapy.

There are at least two conceptual pitfalls in this kind of thinking. For one thing, as we have already seen, an examination of the communication that goes on between any two selected parts of a system is often misleading because it disregards the state of the total system. Any communicative exchange between two persons may be a fragment of a larger picture that cannot be discovered by observing only the two speakers. Second, when we observe any given sequence of acts, the *meaning* of the observed sequence is always in question. As Morton Deutsch (1954) once commented, "if two persons A and B are running one behind the other, it may mean that either A is leading B or that B is chasing A" (p. 187).

Watzlawick, Beavin, and Jackson (1967) discussed how a similar sort of uncertainly about sequence occurs in many verbal exchanges, calling it a problem of "punctuation," where the interpretation of what is stimulus and what is response is perceived differently by each participant. Such disagreement, they noted, is at the root of countless family fights, as illustrated in Diagram 1.1, a graphic representation of a classic marital battle between a "nagging" wife and a "passive" husband. The wife claims, "I only nag because you withdraw," and the husband claims, "I withdraw because you nag." (The starting point is arbitrary.) Obviously each believes that the other causes their fights (Watzlawick, Beavin, & Jackson, 1967, pp. 56–57).

In this illustration, the husband sees only the action triads 2–3–4, 4–5–6, 6–7–8, and 8–9–10; that is, he sees himself as only responding to her actions. The wife sees only 1–2–3, 3–4–5, 5–6–7, 7–8–9, and 9–10–11; that is, she sees herself as simply responding to his actions. The transactional perspective would hold that neither husband nor wife in this sequence provides either the stimulus for the other's behavior or the response to it, but that each is equally a part of the system that produces such an uninterrupted sequence of behaviors.

In addition to influencing the way we will look at family communication in this book, the transactional principle

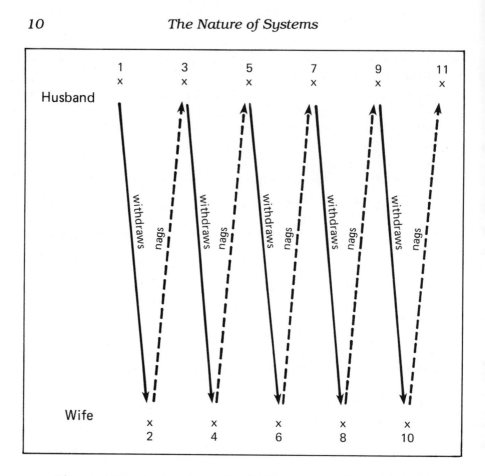

Diagram 1.1. A classic marital battle between "nagging" wife and "passive" husband. From P. Watzlawick, J. Beavin, & D. D. Jackson (1967), *Pragmatics of Human Communication.* New York: Norton. With permission of the publisher.

raises questions about the simple cause-effect relationships often described between any two ingredients in a family situation, such as: The child failed in school because of his low IQ; or, the mother's fears caused her child to be neurotic; or, the husband's excessive drinking caused a divorce.

Following the transactional principle, there is an error in thinking that the relationship between any two things exists without taking into account how other elements of the system interact with each other. Factors such as IQ scores or anxiety or alcoholic consumption are meaningless unless they are considered as part of the total field. As applied to the family, this also suggests that rather than searching for one-to-one causal relationships (as parent-affecting-child or husband-affecting-wife), we could more profitably look for such global processes as total relational configurations, family rule systems, coalitions, and interaction patterns that include the whole family.

HOLISM

The view of the family as a system has still another root in the currently popular view known as "holism," which, in the medical field, stresses the importance of considering the whole person, in the belief that no part of the person can be fully understood except within the context of the total person. Not only does holism view the organism as a totality, but it also sees the individual as an interacting component with its environment. The interpenetration of the organism and its culture is so complex that the two cannot be unraveled, and to try to do so destroys the natural unity of the whole.

The term *holism* was coined in 1925 by General J. C. Smuts, who believed that matter, life, and mind co-exist and mingle in the human being, and that the three are genetically related. While once looked on with suspicion by the medical profession, this notion has been adopted by many respected health professionals who treat the patient as a totality, rather than treating the symptoms. Somewhat reminiscent of Lewin's second principle of field theory, holistic practioners point out that although the whole is indeed made up of parts, these parts cannot be separated and then examined or treated separately without drastically affecting the functioning of other parts, and of the whole.

Viewing the family holistically is not a new idea; as early as 1926 Ernest Burgess was describing the family as "as unity of interacting personalities," (1968, pp. 28–34), but it was not until the mid-1950s that this idea was given serious attention. Here the impetus came from psychotherapy, where psychiatrists had previously treated their patients alone, believing it was poor technique for therapists to have any contact with their patient's family. Even when some practitioners began to recognize that the mother often played an important part in the emotional sickness of her child, the child was still regarded as an innocent victim of a bad mother. Further discoveries were soon made, however, suggesting that an inadequate *father* also contributed to a child's disturbance, that the various *sibling* relations were part of the clinical picture, and even the identified patient was actively participating in his or her own sickness. Thus, only gradually did full recognition come that the mental illness of one member is only a symptom of an interlocking family pathology. Today we assume that a healthy family—one without an emotionally disturbed or delinquent member—also functions holistically. Unfortunately we know far less about how the healthy whole-family interacts because there has been less motivation for studying it. In later chapters, we will take a closer look at specific interaction patterns observed in families with a disturbed member, who, in the holistic view, is only a symptom of the family dysfunction.

GENERAL SYSTEM THEORY

Another holistic view, and one that is crucial to our present study of the family, is general system theory (GST). Like field theory, GST had its origins in gestalt psychology and the work of Max Wertheimer, Wolfgang Kohler, and Kurt Koffka in Germany. The gestalt principle upon which GST is based states unequivocally that the analysis of parts or components cannot provide an understanding of the functioning whole. Originally applied to the natural sciences, GST today, through the work of von Bertalanffy, includes psychology, the social sciences, and other behavioral sciences under its broad theoretical umbrella.

General system theory represents a search for universal

principles that apply to all systems, without regard for the specific nature, components, or purposes of any particular system. For example, laws applicable to physics or biology might equally well apply to economics and psychology. Although based on mathematics and closely linked with computer science, GST actually provides a broad view, a view which, in von Bertalanffy's words, "is operative, with varying degrees of success and exactitude, in various realms" (1968, p. xii).

In searching for structural similarities (or *isomorphies*) in different fields, there is some danger that superficial analogies can cause us to overlook actual differences. Therefore, as von Bertalanffy warned, this approach must be used with some caution:

> General system theory is not a search for vague and superficial analogies. Analogies as such are of little value since besides similarities between phenomena, dissimilarities can always be found as well. The isomorphism under discussion is more than mere analogy. It is a consequence of the fact that in certain respects, corresponding abstractions and conceptual models can be applied to different phenomena. Only in view of these aspects will system laws apply. This is not different from the general procedure in science. It is the same situation as when the law of gravitation applies to Newton's apple, the planetary system and tidal phenomena. This means that in view of certain limited aspects a theoretical system, that of mechanics, holds true; *it does not mean that there is a particular resemblance between apples, planets, and oceans in a great number of other aspects.* (1968, pp. 35–36)

Taking care, then, to avoid misleading analogies that may imply more sameness than is warranted, we can now look at some selected general system principles that seem particularly relevant to families, and will later consider some specific applications of these principles in family systems.

The Principle of Fundamental Unity

This principle holds that the universe is one massive system which can be viewed as being composed of any number of given subsystems. However, it is also appropriate to view any subsystem as a system in its own right, provided we take into account that system's "environment," or the next greater system (suprasystem) of which that system is a part.

System Change

As we have stressed before, a system by definition is not an assemblage of independent components. Thus the character of a system cannot be known simply by knowing the nature of its various parts. However, the character of a system *is* influenced by each of its parts, for whenever a part or a relationship between parts changes, the entire system is re-formed. This means that a system is not created gradually by the addition of parts, but exists instantly and can instantly undergo transformation. Any addition, loss, or functional change in a part will cause changes in the number and kind of interrelationships, thus instantly creating a new system. Change can come about because of a shifting of components or relationships *within* the system (*first order* change) or because new information enters the system from *outside* the system boundaries (*second order* change). As we will see later, this is a significant difference when attempting to bring about therapeutic change in a disturbed family system.

Viability

Any healthy system acts in such a way as to maintain itself and remain alive (or *viable*). In biology, viability means the ability of an organism to live and grow by producing new cells to replace those lost. In similar way, a social system remains viable only so long as it continues to change and reform, creating successive *new states*, while at the same time maintaining the boundaries that make it a system. It ac-complishes this through various "rules" that permit the system to remain open to new environmental inputs, to regulate itself, and to adjust collectively to the stress it encounters. Strictly speaking, however, a system that loses its viability does not *die*, it simply breaks up, becoming more and more random in its behavior until it can no longer be regarded as a system. In system terms, such an increase in randomness, or disorder, is called *entropy*. Thus, an increase in entropy means a decrease in order or structure in the system, and the system with high entropy moves more rapidly toward a random state.

Open and Closed Systems

It will helpful at this point to distinguish between open systems and closed systems, since these terms have a special meaning in systems theory and will be used frequently in the chapters that follow. As already seen, any system is subject to a succession of different states, and the transitions from one state to another are called "transformations." When these transformations involve no new material or information, but simply have to do with the rearrangement of bits of information already present within the system's boundary, the system is called *closed* (Beer, 1964, p. 41). (Note that the only change possible in a closed system is first order change.) In contrast, an open system maintains itself by a constant process of input and output. The closed system is cut off from its environment and seeks to keep a state of equilibrium within its boundaries. The open system, because of its constant exchange of information and energy with the outside environment, is never in a state of lasting equilibrium, but by adapting to new inputs may attain a series of "steady states." The steady state of an open system is not reversible, but represents a succession of adjustments to constantly changing inputs (Bertalanffy, 1968, p. 39). A machine is a closed system, but any *living* organism is essentially an open system and cannot remain viable for long without some contact with its environment.

Every system has a tendency to "run down" over time as its energy flow becomes less structured and more disordered. This tendency toward disorder or randomness—entropy—

occurs more rapidly in a system that has few inputs from outside its boundary—a more restricted energy supply, so to speak. A closed system tends to run down because it is cut off from an exchange of energy with its surroundings, whereas an open system resists running down because it interacts with the environment, giving and receiving energy (Cherry, 1961, p. 215). It is important to recognize, too, that an open system means not only that it has interchanges with the environment, but that this interchange is an *essential factor* underlying the system's viability (Buckley, 1967, p. 50).

System Boundaries

In a simplified view, we can picture every system as having a boundary that defines the relationships and events that exist within the boundary as being somehow different from those that exist outside it. The boundary can also serve the purpose of a filter, in that it permits or inhibits energy from entering or leaving the system. Boundaries also exist *between* subsystems and can be described along a continuum from permeable to impermeable, depending upon how firm the separation of parts—from totally closed off from one another to such blurred boundaries that one component seems merged with another, or others.

Homeostasis

A system has the characteristic of seeking to keep itself in a state of balance. This is called *homeostasis and can be explained rather simply as a control device for keeping the behavior of the system within desired limits. Whenever something occurs that it outside the system's acceptable range, the system becomes unbalanced and tension is created. When this happens, the system's homeostatic mechanism is triggered in order to regain its balance. Now the system scans itself, decides what is creating the imbalance, and adjusts itself to a desirable range with subsequent return to a low-tension state.*

Feedback

This is the method by which a system maintains a steady state. When a system gets out of balance, for whatever reason, *positive* feedback will increase its deviation, while *negative* feedback acts as an error-activating process designed to help the system regain a steady state. Thus negative feedback corrects the imbalance and returns the system to a balanced state. Information about malfunctioning in the system (in the form of negative feedback) is therefore essential for change to occur. (Notice that the terms "positive" and "negative" as used in system theory should not be interpreted in the ordinary sense of reward and punishment. Negative feedback is simply an impetus for change, while positive feedback is not.)

Feedback then is the term used to describe the process of scanning and regulating. It is customarily illustrated by the common room thermostat, which constantly "scans" the room temperature and directs the heating or cooling mechanisms to turn on whenever the temperature varies significantly from an acceptable point. This kind of feedback mechanism is an example of a system with a narrow range of acceptable behavior. For example, if the thermostat is set at 72°, the heat could be set to turn on if the room temperature falls to 71° (negative feedback) and the cooling apparatus could be activated if the temperature rises to 73°. In other kinds of systems, including social systems, the acceptable range may be very wide, but in any event there is some point at which negative feedback would cause the system to begin to take self-correcting action. If not, the system rapidly become disordered. Some systems, because of looser homeostatic controls, have a wider range of acceptable behavior, so the system shows greater behavioral variation, fewer rules, greater tendency toward disorder. It is possible, then, to identify a system's general character in terms of its feedback-based homeostatic controls, as (1) flexible, (2) rigid, or (3) disordered.

We will see later how this classification might also apply to families.

Equifinality

An open system demonstrates greater flexibility than a closed system in the way it processes inputs. In machine-like systems, the movement from input to output follows a fixed path, where one input produces one and only one output. In a less mechanistic system, the final output may be achieved through a variety of different routes. If one route is closed, or one component fails to function, alternate routes and components are available. In other words, the same goal may be reached in different ways. This is the principle of *equifinality*: that many different processes can lead to the same results (Bertalanffy, 1968). A telephone system is an example of an inflexible system with low equifinality, and the human brain is an example of a system with *high* equifinality. Colin Cherry contrasts the two extremes:

> There is, first, the remarkable fact that large portions of the cortex may be cut away (except the speech areas), often with little or no effect upon memory, personality, or intelligence. But in telephone exchanges each wire has a unique function, and destruction of any part has a permanent and serious result. To make another simile, if we imagine a great library containing books which have a vast number of cross-references one to another, then should one whole shelf be burned, it might be possible to reconstruct the lost books—but somewhat less perfectly than at first. There would be great structural redundancy; and the brain appears to possess such safety factors to an immense degree. (1961, p. 300)

Families, too, seem to have this factor to an immense degree, but in inflexible family systems, the factor is severely restricted, as we shall see later.

Interconnectivity

Under conditions of stress, a system either concentrates the strain on one selected point or may distribute the stress throughout the entire system. Obviously, in the latter case, the system can bear more, because the collective strength of the entire system is brought into play. The analogy of an old-fashioned cot, strung with a network of interlinking wires, is appropriate; a weight heavy enough to snap any single wire could be placed on this interlocked network in such a way that the wire that could not support eighty pounds alone is able to bear over one thousand pounds because it is part of an interconnected system. For interconnectivity to exist, a system must be well-structured. Without sufficient structure, disorganization and eventually chaos occurs; *with* adequate structure, the system displays a congruent interdependence, whereby all components function together.

The Family System: Some Analogies

If the family is indeed a system, it follows that the system attributes discussed earlier are equally applicable to it. This chapter will consider how system principles can be interpreted in terms of the family. As Bertalanffy warned, we should not attempt to push the analogies too far, but instead should seek for true isomorphies where they exist.

SUBSYSTEMS AND SUPRASYSTEMS IN FAMILIES

We believe that the family can best be understood as a totality. However, following the principle of fundamental unity, it is also true that each member is also a system. The individual system exists within a greater system that can be identified as the nuclear family, which exists within a still greater system (*suprasystem*) of the extended family, the tribe, or the community. This, in turn, exists within a state or nation, and so on until we theoretically reach some universal social system. This book is primarily concerned with events that occur within the boundary of the nuclear family, but we must remain aware that the family is a subsystem of society and as such interacts to some extent with the greater systems that encompass it.

As we saw earlier, subsystems are systems within systems, and within the family, membership in subsystems usually overlaps. That is, each family member may be a part of several subsystems at the same time. A woman may belong to a marital subsystem with her husband, a parent-child subsystem with her child, and a child-parent subsystem with her own mother, all within the framework of the family system.

Since the behavior of a family, like that of all systems, is dynamic, each member has a different set of behaviors that he or she can enact with each other member or combination of members, depending upon which subsystem is involved at any given time. Laing and Esterson (1964) illustrated this with the various "Jills" in one family:

> Let us suppose that Jill has a father and mother and brother, who all live together. If one wishes to form a complete picture of her as a family person ... it will be necessary to see how she experiences and acts in all the following contexts:
> Jill alone.
> Jill with mother.
> Jill with father.
> Jill with brother.
> Jill with mother and father.
> Jill with mother and brother.
> Jill with father and brother.
> Jill with mother, father, and brother. (p. 20)

This means that Jill's behavior can be explained or predicted only by knowing the state of her relational field at any given moment. This, of course, complicates the analysis considerably; a simple personality-type analysis would involve the study of only four persons (Jill, mother, father and brother), whereas the system analysis would require the study of at least twelve different relationships because the formula for determining the number of possible relationships in $N(N-1)$, where N = the number of family members, or in the case of Jill's family, 4×3. All the relationships, as well as possible interrelationships of the various groupings create considerable complexity, even if we do not take into account Jill's outside relations based on school, friendships, sports, job, and so on. Because her family's internal subsystems and coalitions also interact with one another as well as with the total family, the matter of internal boundaries between subsystems becomes exceedingly important, as will become evident later on.

HOW FAMILY SYSTEMS CHANGE

Recalling that entire systems can change instantly with the addition or deletion of a single component, consider again the case of Jill-with-mother, which constitutes a different subsystem than does Jill-with-mother-and-father. Suppose, for example, that Jill and her mother are talking together and her father appears and joins the two. The Jill-mother dyad has become a triad and its interactions may undergo immediate change, either in an effort to include the father or to form a two-against-one coalition. In another context, consider also how the birth of a new baby alters the existing relationships in a family: the mother and father do not relate to each other in precisely the same way as before (some couples even begin to call each other "Mom" or "Dad"); an older child is no longer the baby, and sibling relations may undergo dramatic changes, with new splits and alliances being formed. Events such as death or divorce are better understood if seen as creating a totally new system by altering previous relationships. In much the same way, as a child grows up and leaves home, the mother's emotional upheaval may be more intense than the event would seem to warrant, unless we understand that the mother not only has "lost" a child, but must also adjust to a totally new system. How the family deals with change—that is, whether it seeks a new stable state based on changed circustances, or whether it strives to retain the old system, unchanged at any cost—is an important determinant of family health.

OPEN AND CLOSED FAMILY SYSTEMS

A family, because it is a living organism, is necessarily an open system to some extent. Also, following the principle of fundamental unity, we know that no family can be totally closed because it is always embedded in some greater system and must interact with it in some way, although contact may be minimal. To be completely accurate, we should describe family systems in terms of varying degrees of openness. For convenience, however, the family that has very little outside contact will be referred to as *closed.*

The Closed Family

A family is a closed system according to the above inter-pretation when it isolates itself, physically or psychologically, from the community in which it resides. Its members may have limited contacts outside the immediate family and may tend to "cloister" themselves, withdrawing from the demands of a society that they may fear they cannot meet. Such a family may have strongly enforced rules that keep its members markedly different from other families, or may build rigid boundaries that restrict both input and output of infor-mation. They display what has been called a "closed circuit" (Elles, 1967).

Kantor & Lehr (1975), in their book about family systems, postulated that in a closed family system even the social and physical space is rigidly fixed by authority, as is the regulation of incoming/outgoing traffic. The describe this control as an aspect of *bounding*:

> Bounding, the social space mechanism for regulating incoming and outgoing traffic, is carried out by those designated as authorities by the family in such a way that the family's discrete space, distinct and apart from the larger community space is created. Locked doors, careful scrutiny of strangers in the neighborhood, parental control over the media, supervised excursions, and unlisted telephones are all features of a closed-type family. Closed bounding goals include the preservation of territoriality, self-protection, privacy, and in some families, secretiveness. (pp. 119–120)

This matter of family secrets in closed families is one of considerable import, as we will see later when discussing severe family pathologies in Chapter 7. Closed families, in addition to resisting what they see as an invasion of outside ideas and feelings, may guard their own secrets from the outside community, presenting only a public image or certain carefully manufactured myths about themselves. The need to support and keep alive these myths is a potential source of family pathology.

Overinvolvement in the Closed Family

In addition to a closed family's primary feature of cutting itself off from outside influences, there are also other characteristics that make it different from open families. One of the most significant of these is the quality of overinvolvement of members. As we have seen, a family has external boundaries that, in a closed system, tend to lack permeability; a family also has *internal* boundaries that serve to separate subsystems within the family. When subsystem boundaries, separating members from one another, are blurred or non-existent, members are over-involved and their relationships are marked by excessive "togetherness" and absence of personal privacy, with eventual loss of individual autonomy. This is the condition that has been called "fusion" or "merger" or "enmeshment" or "lack of differentiation" in a family—a pathological state that will be treated more fully in later chapters.

Inflexibility in the Closed Family

A third aspect of closed families is that of *rigidity*, or lack of flexibility. This quality is apparent in the closed family's relationships, its communication patterns, and in its homeostatic processes.

Within the closed family little change is permitted, so it is frequently noted to have relationships that rigidify, remaining essentially the same over long periods of time: a 30-year-old son continues to live at home in the role of "mother's little boy;" a middle-aged wife remains as childlike and dependent upon her husband as she was at eighteen; an adolescent girl permits herself to be dressed, groomed, and made up by her mother like a big doll (Laing, 1961, p. 84), or an infant-mother symbiosis persists into the "infant's" adolescence, or even later, never permitting essential separation-individuation to occur.

Communication in a closed system is also rigid, mechanical and predetermined ("I knew he'd say that...") and members tend to speak for one another ("What she means to say is..."), often finishing each other's sentences and replying in fixed ways, lacking flexibility and spontaneity. Communication is limited to prescribed topics, and taboo subjects are common. The outer boundary is no longer simply a filter; it has become a barrier, and the system has begun to feed upon itself.

Interaction in closed family systems is sometimes limited to "games without end," because the system's boundary shuts out new information. Without new data the system lacks the capacity to change its own rules, and may continue to recycle information and repeat the same interaction sequences and patterns.

An inflexible-closed family system typically shows a narrowed range of behaviors that members can use in responding to particular situations—to express affection, to deal with anger, to avoid conflicts, and so on. Absence or severe limitation of choice is possibly the most common characteristic of a closed-inflexible system; even when other alternative behaviors are clearly available, members may behave *as if* it were impossible for them to do things differently (in system terms, you will recall that this is a lack of *equifinality*). In such families, patterns of interaction among members appear to resemble a recording—once turned on, it must be played through to its predictable and inevitable end. This is especially true of family arguments which, in an inflexible system, have a here-we-go-again quality, usually displaying a pattern of mutual recrimination and mutual defense. The following selection from the report of a family study (Stachowiak, 1970) illustrates how this might sound. The study involves a family that had applied for assistance for their ten-year-old daughter, who stuttered and was extremely shy. In a family-decision-making experiment, which included the parents, the daughter, and a 12-year-old brother, the following sequence was observed:

> In the experimental situation, it was noted that the daughter attempted to respond to a question. Before she finished her brother "jokingly" responded, "Ah, shut up!" The father told the son to "lay off your sister," and the mother followed this by reprimanding the father for always "picking on" the son. Ther followed a period of awkward silence, and, of course, the daughter never did complete what she started to say. The point to be stressed here is that even though this interaction sequence was repeated several times (with minor variations) during the course of the experiment, the family members were unaware of the nature of the "chain response" and its consequences. (p. 121)

If a family has become rigidified in such a sequencing and patterning of interaction, it is sometimes the role of a family therapist to *destabilize* the family or create disequilibrium in the system by forcing a change in such interaction patterns. This technique is discussed further in Part IV when we look at various models of family therapy.

The Open Family

A family system is called *open* when it is able to change and re-form, creating successive new states, while at the same time maintaining the boundaries that make it a system. Because it is able to delay entropy better than a closed system, the open system is likely to have great viability. It is able to make both first-order changes (recycling of information within the system) *and* second-order changes (changes based on the introduction of new data from outside the system). Its open state is maintained by family rules, usually unstated, which permit the system to remain open to new environmental inputs, to regulate itself, and to adjust collectively to the stresses it encounters.

Outside Contact and Change

Kantor and Lehr (1975) describe how an open-type family functions in respect to outside contact:

> Numerous guests, frequent visits with friends, unlocked doors, open windows, individual or group exploration of the community and its resources, and a freedom of informational exchange with only rare censorship of the media are all bounding features. In general, open bounding fosters the desire for benficial interchange with members of the community, since guests are not only welcome but made to feel important for the contributions they make to the family.
>
> Closeness is encouraged, but temporary distancing is permitted to relieve undue discomfort from too much closeness....Each member is free to establish his own movements toward other members or toward targets, as long as he stays within the guidelines established by family consensus....In its linking strategies, the open family attempts to affirm both collective cohesion and individual freedom. (p. 127)

Flexibility

In addition to its basic characteristic of outside contact, the open-family system typically displays more flexibility than does a closed system. Because each member is permitted greater role versatility, the family has a greater number of alternative routes to replace those lost or disrupted. Even such drastic happenings as death or prolonged separation of members do not cause a flexible-open family structure to collapse. With greater equifinality, flexible families could be expected to have greater viability than inflexible ones; however this system analogy should not be pushed too far, because there is some indication that rigid inflexibility of a family's patterns may provide what Gregory Bateson calls a "tough durability," although this is generally achieved at the expense of individual members.

Connectivity

A third aspect of the open family is that it has the capacity to interconnect without becoming overinvolved or enmeshed. As noted earlier, an open family, by joining together, can cope with stress in a united fashion, absorbing blows that would overwhelm a single member. By contrast, a family with weak interconnections (i.e., a "disengaged" family) may fragment under conditions of strain because members are already separated from one another by impermeable internal boundaries. Such a family may never have learned to solve problems collectively or to deal with each other empathically. Rather, each separate member must cope with problems in his or her own isolated way, often unsuccessfully. The loosely connected family remains unsupportive, perhaps hostile, in its interrelations; the family seems to be held together by rules that restrict behavior and keep members out of one another's way, but does little to help members cope with their own reality. Because such a family lacks structure, it is unable to function congruently.

A strong sense of connection among family members should not be confused, however, with the total togetherness found in the pathologically enmeshed families which are composed of members with little autonomy or differentiation. Although both sorts of families (the interconnected and the enmeshed) may be referred to as "close-knit," the dynamics are quite different, as one represents strong connections between autonomous individuals, while the other suggests fusion, with a weakening or loss of individual feelings of identity.

The enmeshed families, under conditions of stress, do not connect in a healthy way, but may form internal alliances that split the family into hostile coalitions, such as young-against-old or males-against-females. Rigidly enmeshed families in particular have been observed as tending to "break up into warring factions," as a prelude to the selection of a single member to be a scapegoat (Ackerman, 1967, pp. 48–57), who apparently serves the ancient purpose of "drawing off onto himself all the evil influences that beset the tribe." Although the practice of scapegoating is clearly destructive to the member selected for prejudicial treatment, it seems to provide a way for the family to deal with stress without fragmenting. Later, in Chapter 7 we will see more of the practice of scapegoating as it occurs in seriously pathological families.

FAMILY HOMEOSTASIS AND FEEDBACK

All family systems have a self-stabilizing control mechanism that follows the principle of homeostasis, and the functioning of this mechanism seems related to a system's character of being open or closed.

The proper functioning of any homeostatic mechanism depends upon accurate communication of information entering the system. The room thermostat without a thermometer will never "know" when to turn on or off in order to regulate room temperature. Similarly, the family system may have little information from outside itself and therefore lack the capacity for proper assessment and self-regulation. Perhaps worse, the internal communicative processes within a family may be so distorted that no clear messages in the form of feedback or remedial action can be generated.

In an open-family system, the principle of homeostasis does not imply sameness or reversibility to a prior state; it simply means the capacity of the family to adjust to changing conditions by finding a new balance that still falls within an acceptable range. By contrast, the homeostatic process in a closed family demands that the system remain the same (status quo) or return to an earlier state, in order for the system's balance to be maintained. If absolute sameness cannot be achieved—for instance, if a sick member begins to get better—then the closed family may seek a substitute to serve the same purpose of permitting the family to remain essentially unchanged. Thus second-order change is unlikely. As family theorist Ivan Boszormenyi-Nagy noted:

> Family therapists began to get some inkling of the inter-
> locking, homeostatic system of the family and how, in
> extremely intricate fashion, the intrapsychic struggles
> were blended into a transactional whole. *If one family
> member got better, another one had to balance the system
> and get sick* (italics added) (Boszormenyi-Nagy & Framo,
> 1965, p. xvii)

Here are some clincial episodes illustrating how the homeostatic principle may work in a closed family system:

Example #1: A family has a "good" child and a "bad" child. The good child is quiet, well-mannered, and never needs correction. The bad child is rebellious and insolent, in constant trouble with teachers and juvenile authorities. Given special treatment, the bad child begins to reform and become more manageable. Now the former good child reverses his/her role and becomes wild, rebellious and delinquent. (Assumption: the family system requires the presence of a bad child to maintain its homeostatic balance).

Example #2: A family reported of itself, "We are always happy and love one another devotedly." In a therapy session, one member admitted being unhappy and sometimes feeling hostility toward his mother. The family promptly dropped out of therapy, identified the deviant member as "sick," and sent him for individual treatment with another therapist. (Assumption: the family system needed the myth of perpetual happiness and acted to defend itself against exposure of the myth).

Example #3: A husband urged his wife to seek professional help because of her sexual "frigidity." After several months of treatment she felt less sexually inhibited, whereupon her husband become impotent (Jackson, 1970, p. 10). (Assumption: the marriage system required the wife's frigidity to explain and perpetuate their pattern of sexual dysfunction.)

Example #4: A teenage girl tried to tell her parents that she had sexual thoughts and masturbated. They simply told her that she did not. Whenever the subject came up, they repeated that she did not have any thoughts of that kind and did not engage in any such activity (Laing & Esterson, 1964, p. 42). (Assumption: the family's homeostatic balance was upset because the daughter's reported behavior and thoughts were outside the family's acceptable range. They had no mechanism for preventing the unacceptable thoughts and acts, so they simply rejected the information, thus restoring balance to the system).

In a closed family system, if a member creates imbalance by either challenging the family rules or questioning its myths, that member must be "converted." If this fails, that member must be discredited by being made to feel that she/he is evil, or perhaps crazy. If none of these methods work, the disruptive member may be removed from the system in some way. Even the family's attempt to get psychiatric help may be seen as a homeostatic mechanism to restore balance, as Ferreira (1963) observed:

> In fact, the rush to a psychiatrist may constitute a last-ditch attempt to maintain the status quo and re-establish the previous steady state. The family as a whole may then come to expect that the psychiatrist will help them to retain the formula of their relationship, the myth that until now everyone shared and maintained. (p. 459)

It is important to understand—and this will be stressed throughout the book—that the homeostatic function does not *cause* pathology or symptoms in a family member, nor is the indentified patient the innocent victim of processes within his or her family. This would be making the mistake of thinking in terms of linear causality rather than transactionalism, as explained in Chapter 1. Bateson (1959) in an early study of schizophrenic processes, warned of this kind of faulty thinking when he noted that families of schizophrenics were

> ... not simply homeostatic around the invalid status of the particular identified patient ... It is not that at all costs the identified patient must be kept confused; rather it seems as if the patient himself is an accessory—even a willing sacrifice—to the family homeostasis. If he chooses not to play this role there is a likelihood that some other member of the family will assume it in his place. Like many complex homeostatic systems, the pathogenic family seems to be able, like a newt, to regenerate a missing limb. (pp. 128–219)

Summary of
"The Family as System"

Part I has considered the nature of systems and has suggested ways in which it seems appropriate to regard the family as a system. We have discussed field theory, holism, and transactionalism as forerunners or parallels of general system theory and have pointed out some isomorphies that exist between GST and the family, especially with regard to the systems concepts of fundamental unity, viability, feedback, homeostasis, equifinality, interconnectivity, and openness.

Like any other system, a family system can be considered *open* if its outer boundaries are permeable, permitting outside influences to penetrate and allowing exchange of energy between inside and outside; when internal boundaries are strong but also permeable, permitting both interconnectedness and member autonomy; when the family's homeostatic function permits it to seek a constantly changing steady state without striving to maintain the status quo or to return to some earlier state; when its feedback is accurate, its presentation to the world authentic, and its interaction flexible and spontaneous. In contradistinction to an open system, in which members are moderately involved and processes moderately flexible, there appear to be three other theoretically possible types of system that represent extreme positions with regard to involvement and flexibility. These are:

the *closed* system, which by definition has relatively impermeable external boundaries and in which members are likely to be overinvolved because of the system's weak internal boundaries. Such a closed system is also likely to be inflexible (rigid) in other aspects of its functioning, including its communication patterns and its homeostatic processes.

the disordered system, which is characterized by over-flexibility and lack of coherent structure: hence it is subject to excessive instability, unpredictible change, and often chaos.

the *fragmented* or disengaged family system, whose members are only minimally connected with each other. This type of system is underinvolved, with rigid and impermeable internal boundaries.

In the chapters that follow, we will see these same four family styles repeated when we consider a family's communication, its relationships, and its response patterns.

This is a book about families, but is is also about communication. Part II will continue to treat the family as a system, but will also look at applications of communication theory to the family system.

Communication is at the very heart of any system; it not only spells out the boundaries of the system, but also defines the relationships that can exist within the system. Communication is the means by which existing relationships are maintained and also the way in which they are changed and new relationships formed. Communication is ultimately the source of any family's viability, for it is what binds the system together. When communication goes astray, the boundaries are weakened; when communication ceases, the system no longer exists. Because communication is holistic, dynamic, and rule-governed, it too is a system and will be examined more closely in the following chapters, when we consider how a family makes meaning together.

REFERENCES

Ackerman, N. W. (1967). Prejudice and scapegoating in the family. In Zuk, G. E. & Boszormenyi-Nagy (Eds.), *Family Therapy and Disturbed Families*. pp. 48–57. Palo Alto: Science & Behavior Books.

Bateson, G. (1959). Cultural problems posed by a study of schizophrenic processes. In Auerbach, A. (Ed.), *Schizophrenia: An Integrated Approach*. New York: Ronald Press.

Beer, S. (1964). *Cybernetics and Management*. New York: John Wiley.

Bertalanffy, L. von (1968). *General System Theory: Foundations, Development, Applications*. New York: Braziller.

Birdwhistell, R. L. (1959). Contributions of linguistic and kinesic studies to the understanding of schizophrenia. In Auerbach, A. (Ed.), *Schizophrenia: An Integrated Approach*, pp. 99–123. New York: Ronald Press.

Boszormenyi-Nagy, I., & Framo, J. L. (1965). *Intensive Family Therapy*. Hagerstown, Md.: Harper.

Bowen, M. (1978). *Family Therapy in Clinical Practice*. New York: Gardner Press.

Buckley, W. (1967). *Sociological and Modern Systems Theory*. Englewood Cliffs, N. J.: Prentice-Hall.

Burgess, E. (1968). The family as a unity of interacting personalities. In Heiss, J. (Ed.), *Family Roles and Interaction*, pp. 28–34. Chicago: Rand McNally.

Cherry, C. (1961). *On Human Communication*. New York: Science Editions.

Deutsch, M. (1954). Field theory in social psychology. In Lindzey, G. (Ed.), *Handbook of Social Psychology*, pp. 180–197. Cambridge, Mass.: Addison-Wesley.

Dewey, J., & Bentley, A. F. (1949). *Knowing and the Known*. Boston: Beacon Hill Press.

Elles, G. W. (1967). The closed circuit: The study of a delinquent family. In Handel, G. (Ed), *The Psychosocial Interior of the Family*, pp. 206–219. Chicago: Aldine.

Ferreira, A. J. (1963). Family myth and homeostasis, *Archives of General Psychiatry, 9*, 457–463.

Haley, J. (1967). The family of the schizophrenic: A model system. In Handel, G. (Ed.), *The Psychosocial Interior of the Family*, pp. 251–274. Chicago: Aldine.

Jackson, D. D. (1970). The question of homeostasis. In Jackson, D. D. (Ed.), *Communication, Family and Marriage*, pp. 1–21. Palo Alto: Science & Behavior Books.

Kantor, D., & Lehr, W. (1975). *Inside the Family*. San Francisco: Jossey-Bass.

Laing, R. D. (1961) *Self and Others*. New York: Random House.

Laing, R. D., & Esterson, A. (1964): *Sanity, Madness and the Family*. London: Tavistock Publications/Penguin; New York: Basic Books.

Lederer, W. J., & Jackson, D. D. (1968). *The Mirages of Marriage*. New York: Norton.

Lewin, K. (1951). *Field Theory in the Social Sciences*. New York: Harper.

Satir, V. (1972). *Peoplemaking*. Palo Alto: Science & Behavior Books.

Stachowiak, J. G. (1970). Decision-making and conflict resolution in the family group. In Larson, C. E. & Dance, F. E. X. (Eds.), *Perspectives on Communication*, pp. 113-124. Shorewood, Wisc.: Helix Press.

Vogel, E. F., & Bell, N. W. (1967). The emotionally disturbed child as the family scapegoat. In Handel, G. (ed.), *The Psychosocial Interior of the Family*, pp. 424–442. Chicago: Aldine.

Watzlawick, P., Beavin, J., & Jackson, D. D. (1967). Pragmatics of Human Communication. New York: Norton.

PART II

THE COMMUNICATION PERSPECTIVE

CHAPTER

3

The Process of Making Meaning

In the last chapter we looked at the family as a complex of interacting components, and saw that in a number of respects a family behaves in accordance with principles that govern any system. Because a system is linked together by some form of communication among its various parts, and because the system as a whole is also linked to some degree with the world outside its boundaries, we will in this chapter take a look at how such linking occurs—or how meaning is made—and with what consequences.

In addition to being an essential element of the family system, the process of communication is itself a system. We say this because communication is not self-contained, but requires sender-receiver-environment interaction, and because it is always transactional, thus an open system. Even though we may sometimes feel that we are "talking to

39

ourselves," research suggests that even silent communication (verbal thought) is in reality addressed to some imaginary other. The Russian psychologist A. R. Luria found that children often engage in internal speech, but that this occurs because the child internalizes some partner who, although not physically present, is imagined. Of this aspect Brown and Keller (1973) wrote:

> Internal speech, or *verbal thought*, if you like, develops as the child internalizes the partner who is not present, a feat which depends upon, as a first stage, imagining he is talking to another person--best done when he has somebody present. In this way a child turns himself into the recipient of his own message. (p. 185)

Scholars in many disciplines are concerned with meaning and have struggled with the philosophical "meaning of meaning"—linguists, semanticists, and cultural anthropologists, to mention only a few. There are at least as many interpretations of meaning as there are disciplines that deal with language (Osgood, Suci, & Tannenbaum, 1961, p. 284), but in this chapter we will consider only those aspects of meaning that relate to the encoding and decoding of messages, with related emotional responses. This is the special domain of the communication theorist.

It is customary to begin any discussion of human communication by saying that it involves the sending and receiving of messages. Actually this view invites oversimplification because it fails to take into account the transactional properties of communication. The process can be more easily understood if we try to forget the notion that meaning can be *sent* from one person to another, or *transferred* from one mind to another. The word "evoke" has been suggested as more accurate than "send" or "transmit" because it expresses the active role that both sender and receiver play in the making of meaning. It is also important to emphasize that meaning does not reside solely in the mind of a speaker, nor in the words used, nor in the things (referents) that the words stand for, nor even in the mind of the person who interprets the words, but occurs as a consequence of a complex series of transactions among all these elements. Barnlund (1962) has used "creation of meaning" to refer to the entire process, and this seems appropriate for our use in this chapter.

THE IMPOSSIBILITY OF SHARING EXPERIENCE

The first and most obvious obstacle to making meaning with another person is that direct mind-to-mind contact is not possible, or at least not generally believed to be possible. Neither ideas nor emotions are really shared because they are articulated, although we tend to believe that once another person has been told something, then he *knows*. Even allowing for the possibility of telepathic powers, it is not likely that any person can ever experience another's experience; he can only infer by the other's behavior what that person's experience is at any given moment. The behaviors upon which such inferences are based are regarded by communication scholars as only *signals* which, at best, are crudely coded representations of the other's experience—signals that must be translated, or decoded, by the receiver if meaning is to be made.

In a rather general way, we can say that the creation of meaning involves, first, the enactment by one person of some behavior that has significance for the other person and, second, the other's *interpretation* of the signals presented. Meaning thus created is never an exact replication of the other person's experience or even intent. Relatively similar meaning can be made only to the extent that the receiver's interpretation of some behavior *resembles* what it meant to the one who produced the behavior. Totally accurate communication, if possible, would mean that the signals had evoked in the receiver precisely the same emotional and cognitive state as that existing in the sender. However—and this is an important point that will come up again in this and subsequent chapters—even when meaning is less than identical, communication *still occurs* because meaning of some kind is constantly being evoked in others present. Whether the meaning is accurate or inaccurate, intentional or unintentional, is another matter.

THE TECHNICAL PROBLEM OF SIGNAL TRANSMISSION

There are many ways for what we loosely term "communication breakdown" to occur. For one thing, it is possible for the signal to be acoustically imperfect or for it to be interfered with by something else in the environment. This is called the *technical* problem of communication (Shannon & Weaver, 1949), one that is of interest primarily to information theorists or electronic engineers who deal with non-human communication systems. One of the most often used and influential models growing out of this view of communication is that of Claude Shannon and Warren Weaver (1949), engineers for Bell Telephone Company, who conceived of communication as the accurate transmission of information from source to receiver through a series of functions. Their model, originally intended to apply only to mechanical or electronic systems, has been adopted freely by the behavioral sciences and used to describe human interaction (see Diagram 3.1).

Because this model is linear, it is not entirely satisfactory for describing human communication, which we know to be transactional; however it does illustrate one aspect of all communication—the loss or distortion of signals and the introduction of noise. While this does not appear to be a major problem in human interaction, it no doubt contributes to misunderstanding resulting from loss of signal accuracy.

From a technical viewpoint, however, the human receiver appears to be exceedingly efficient, performing feats of reception and recognition of signals that are far beyond the capabilities of our most sophisticated computers, and in the face of extreme interference or weakness of signals. For example, the voice of speakers may be so low that much of

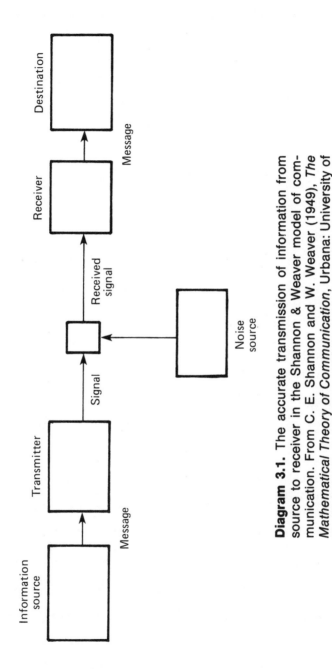

Diagram 3.1. The accurate transmission of information from source to receiver in the Shannon & Weaver model of communication. From C. E. Shannon and W. Weaver (1949), *The Mathematical Theory of Communication*, Urbana: University of Illinois Press, p. 5. With permission of the publisher.

what they say is inaudible to the listener; they may speak with an accent that is unfamiliar; they may talk with a mouth full of food; they may speak from another room or from where their voices are muffled, or they may speak simultaneously with competing noices. In these and other such instances researchers have found that the human subject shows an astonishing capacity to pick up signals with a fair degree of accuracy, following what one speaker says even when others are talking at the same time, and/or filtering out one conersation from a jumble of other sounds and noises. (This has been called the "cocktail party problem," and is one that no machine has yet been able to resolve, although humans can do it quite naturally and easily, piecing together a coherent message from the barest of information.) As telecommunications expert Colin Cherry (1961) noted some years ago, "There are many sources of uncertainty, yet speech communication works" (p. 277). The explanation for most communication problems in human groups, including families, apparently lies elsewhere.

In an effort to make the Shannon and Weaver model more applicable to human communication, it has been converted into human terms, as in the model shown in Diagram 3.2 (Valentine, 1963), demonstrating the following process: (1) An idea, is (2) encoded and translated into language, (3) sent out by a transmitter, (4) as a signal over some particular channel or channels (for example audible and visual), (5) which are invariably disturbed by some noise; (6) the signal and the interfering noise are picked up by a receiver and (7) decoded in some way. Hopefully, an idea similar to that which started the process is stimulated in the mind of the person to whom the communication is addressed (p. 168).

Like all such linear models, however, this one is not entirely satisfactory, not only because it lacks the process of feedback, so essential for understanding communication in transactional terms, but more importantly because it does not show the systemic or holistic aspect of communication. As Peter Drucker (1957) commented:

> It is the whole of speech, including not only the words left unsaid but the whole atmosphere in which words are said

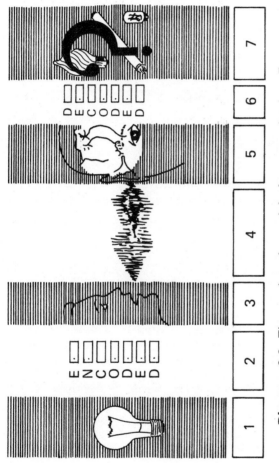

Diagram 3.2. The engineer's model of communication. From M. Valentine (1963), Information theory and the psychology of speech. In J. Eisenson, J. Auer, and V. Irwin, *The Psychology of Communication*, p. 168. New York: Appleton-Century-Crofts. With permission of the publisher.

and heard, that "communicates." One must not only know the whole of the "message," one must also be able to relate it to the pattern of behavior, personality, situation, and even culture with which it is surrounded. (p. 36)

A discussion of many of these holistic concerns will continue in the next section when we consider the problem of decoding, or interpretation.

THE SEMANTIC PROBLEM OF INTERPRETATION

Once the signal has been received, it must then be decoded, or interpeted by the receiver. This is called the "semantic problem of communication" (Shannon & Weaver, 1949)—one that is the source of considerable human difficulty, where message misinterpretation often plays havoc with human relationships.

First, it is clear that the way we interpret messages is a product of our individual learning. As Dean Barnlund (1970) expressed it:

> While we are born into and inhabit a world without meaning, we rapidly invest it with significance and order. That life becomes intelligible to us—full of beauty or ugliness, hope or despair—is because it is assigned that significance by the experiencing being. Sensations do not come to us all sorted and labeled, as if we were visitors in a vast but ordered museum. Each, instead, in his own curator. We learn to look with a selective eye, to classify, to assign significance. (p. 87)

The need to "assign significance" to whatever signals we receive may be further complicated by selective attention, the possibilities of incongruent messages in different modalities (which forces the receiver to decide about conflicting messages), and the tendency toward symbolic manipulations.

The Many Modalities of Meaning

To begin with, meaning is never a single, fixed thing, inherent in a word or act but occurs on multiple levels, along various channels, using many different modalities. The speaker uses words and sentences, but simultaneously moves and positions his body, contracts or relaxes various facial muscles to produce "facial expression," and changes the pitch, stress, and volume of his voice to create different "tones of voice"; all these modalities evoke meaning in the receiver. The physical handling of a baby has meaning for that baby without any regard for words; the intonation of a husband's voice may suggest impatience or disgust to a sensitive wife; the same act may have a different meaning in one context than it does in another (a slap on a child's bottom may be play or punishment to the child, depending on the circumstances—and the parent's accompanying nonverbal behavior). Some modalities are used deliberately with conscious awareness on the part of the sender (such as words and sentences); other modalities may be used *without* the sender's awareness, and may in fact evoke a message quite different from the sender's intent. Moreover, there is no guarantee that the various modalities are in agreement in the meaning they suggest. A speaker may say one thing with words, but "say" quite a different thing with tone of voice, and a still different thing with facial expression or gesture. The message sender may further complicate things by deliberately presenting fraudulent cues intended to conceal or falsify his/her "real" meaning. At the same time, the receiver exercises a power of selection by choosing what s/he will attend to in the total message context, rejecting many of the signals presented and distorting others to make the message fit preconceived expectations, needs, or fantasies. All this will be considered at length in the follow sections.

Selective Attention and Inattention

When messages are misunderstood or missed altogether, it is far more likely to be the result of factors within the receiver's own psychological system than because of technical loss of signal. All living organisms are selective about what they perceive and respond to, continuously reacting to some things in their environment and not responding to others that are just as readily available to them. Even though two communicators share a common language and have had essentially the same experience with one another's verbal and nonverbal signals, there may be little real meaning created between them if each blocks from awareness the other's transmissions. In actuality, each party is *able* to be aware of only a fragment of what the other says and does, as literally thousands of discrete impressions per second impinge on a human being's receptors; some kind of screening is obviously necessary. Psychiatric theorist Harry Stack Sullivan called this screening process "selective inattention," and believed that the basis for each individual's selection is the avoidance of anxiety. According to Sullivan, new data are admitted to awareness only to the extent that they are consistent with data already accepted by the receiver. Information that is inconsistent or uncomfortable is simply excluded, usually by involuntary processes (Sullivan, 1953). This is quite different from sheer perversity or even negligent oversight, although frustrated parents and spouses tend to believe that understanding would magically happen if the other person would only *listen* or *pay attention.*

There appears to be another kind of selectivity which is more deliberate and occurs because each of us learns rather early in life that not everything matters. The young child exercises less selectivity than an older one—as anyone can attest who has ever asked a five-year-old what a movie or television program was *about.* The child may have missed the point of the story, but can give an interminable account of what he saw and heard, with something like total recall of often-irrelevant details. An older child has learned to screen out those things that do not matter. The trouble, of course, is that the older child also tunes out some things that *do* matter, possibly filling the gap with his own projections or fantasies. Considerable selectivity is also exercised by marital partners, especially those of long standing, simply because each has come to believe that s/he knows what the other will do or say.

And each may "hear" or otherwise perceive whatever s/he anticipates from the other, whether or not it ever happens.

Symbols and Symbolic Manipulation*

All communication rests on the premise that things can indicate, or stand for other things. To a dog, the sight and smell of his leash may indicate that he is going outside; a proper name is used to indicate a particular person; tears may indicate the presence of strong emotion; a dark cloud may indicate a coming storm. The process by which one thing can indicate another involves two quite different functions. One of these, common to all animals, including human, is *signification,* or the creation of meaning through use of signs, and the other, believed to be unique in human animals, is based upon the capacity for performing symbolic transformation— for manipulating symbols.

Simply put, *sign* communication serves a function much like pointing: the sign announces the presence of some other thing or condition and directs attention to it, probably without *intent* to communicate. A chimpanzee in the jungle makes a distinctive cry to signify "danger!"; a honeybee wiggles its body in such a way as to signify the distance and direction of honey; the odor of a female mammal in estrus is a sign to which the male of the species will respond with excitement. Each such natural sign points to another thing or event, but it is also linked directly with the thing or condition it signifies, and may be inseparable from it. (For example, the bared fang of a dog is a threatening gesture that has obvious connection with the specific threat it signifies: biting.)

Not all signs are natural. Humans can produce artificial, or arbitrary, signs that intentionally point to or call attention to other things or conditions, usually more important than the sign itself. An alarm clock rings to call attention to the hour; a

---

* The words "sign," "signal," and "symbol" are used rather loosely in the literature. For the most part, each writer is consistent in his or her own way of using these terms, but one writer's sign is another's signal. In general, this discussion follows the usage of Ernst Cassirer and Susanne Langer, also drawing from linguist Roger Brown and anthropologist Gregory Bateson.

red light signifies that traffic is to stop; a buzzer sounds in the automobile to call attention to an unfastened seat belt. These are not natural signs in the same sense that the bared fang represents a part-for-whole coding, but depend instead on learned consensual agreement for their meaning. They do, however, qualify as signs because they serve the limited purpose of all true signs: they call attention to something else in the immediate environment at the immediate moment.

Human beings, in common with all animals, have the capacity to communicate with signs, but they have the additional capacity to use and interpret *symbols*. A symbol, like a sign, stands for something else, but differs in that it is not an integral part of the happening for which it stands, nor is it used simply to call attention to something present at the moment. With symbols, human beings can not only announce the presence of other things, but can also lead others to think about things *not* present, to conceive of things that existed in the past, that are anticipated in the future, or may never have existed at all except in fantasy. A sign is tied to the event it signifies, but a symbol evokes a message *about* the event.

Notice that I am not saying that any given signal is by its nature either a sign or a symbol. The same signals that are used as signs by lower animals may be used by humans in a symbolic way. For instance, a dog may respond to the sound of a familiar name by looking eagerly about for the person named. He is using the word as a sign—an indicator of the immediate presence of the person named. On the other hand, two humans may engage in a conversation *about* a third person not present, using the person's name in a symbolic way that is quite beyond the capacity of a dog. For the two persons, the name does not indicate the presence of the one named, but *represents* him or her and permits them to create an image of the absent person. Similarly, if I pat my dog's head and say gently, "I hate dogs; I think I'll kill you," he will probably wag his tail in delight. He is responding to the tonal and gestural *signs* of my friendliness and good intentions, not to a symbolic image evoked by the words "hate" and "kill." The human being (even a very young one, provided s/he has internalized the language) can respond to both sign meaning and symbol meaning in the same message—and the episode that is quite clear to a dog might create confusion and anxiety in a child who is confronted with conflicting messages. Such *incongruent* messages are a matter of profound significance in the development of human and family pathology, as we will see later.

Emotional Response to Symbols

Symbols derive their meaning—their power to evoke emotional response—through early associations between the symbols (usually words) and other aspects of the situation. Words thus have both denotative meanings that can be gained from the dictionary *and* personal emotional meanings that may be unique to each person. As Virginia Satir (1967) observed, the word "mother" has a *denotative* meaning of a woman who bears and/or rears a child. However, for a person who had a warm, accepting, nurturing mother, the emotional response to the word would be quite different from the response of another who had a cold, demanding, unresponsive mother (p. 64). Two people speaking together of mothers, would hardly be talking about the same thing. Family inter-action abounds with arguments growing out of differing emotional response to symbols associated with money, work, drugs, dress, and sex. Because these are always matters of symbolic response, such arguments can never be resolved by simple intellectual understanding of what the words "mean."

Misreading Signs

Neither signs nor simbols are perfect vehicles for creating meaning because both rely on interpretation. Both animals and humans sometimes simply misinterpret the import of a sign; as Suzanne Langer (1951) noted, "The white rat in a maze makes mistakes and so does the trout who bites at a feather-and-silk fly" (p. 313). So also the human being may misread a printed sign, drive through a red light, or miss a warning sign, but there is even more likelihood of error in mankind's use of symbols. In the following section we will consider some of our more common symbolic "mistakes."

Confusing Sign With Symbol

More significant than the simple misinterpretation of a sign is the human tendency to regard symbols as signs, and to act on them accordingly. This is particularly true in the case of *words*, which are our most important symbols, the basis of our language. Most words, as symbols, are arbitrary, having no necessary meaning, but rather relying on cultural and social custom for their interpretation. There seems to be a rather prevalent belief, however, that words *possess* meaning and that people who share a common language know *the* meaning of each word—or if they don't, they ought to. Consequently people often respond to words *as if* they have unchanging and invariable meanings. There is a measure of truth in this belief because we do learn to interpret words through early inter-action with others, and so they acquire a certain commonality meaning. But this commonality should not blind us to the fact that words are not signs—there is no inherent and necessary connection between word and thing symbolized.

If we make the mistake of confusing sign and symbol, it follows that we may then respond to a symbol as though it were a sign; that is, the signal response is invariable and is performed without fail whenever the symbolic stimulus is presented, as though there were no choice, no alternative response to make, no thought of evaluation. Thus human beings, who should know better, frequently respond to words much as the experimental dogs in Pavlov's studies salivated at the sight of food, and later at the sound of a bell. These persons do not evaluate a response, instead they respond in a pre-determined, rigidly prescribed fashion. We will see more of this later when we discuss family pathologies.

Creating Symbolic "Stories"

The human being's capacity to use symbols means that he or she can create images in his or her own mind and can also evoke images in the minds of others. This image-making power of words is probably the most significant aspect of human verbal communication. Images depend upon symbols because they focus on absent objects; with symbols, people can create elaborate word-pictures of anything they wish. But more than this happens: *the images they create do not remain static, but tend to turn into a changing scene.* As Langer (1951) wrote, "the first thing we do with images is to envisage a story" (p. 158). This tendency to create stories from minimal raw data forms the basis of all the creative, artistic, and inventive accomplishments of the human race. But like some other abilities, it is a mixed blessing, because it is also a source of much miscommunication; for once a person has created a story, s/he may then come to believe it—taking it to be absolute truth, to be preserved and defended, unalterable and unshakable even in the face of contrary evidence. So, as we shall see later, humans come to accept and believe their own models, however distorted they may be. They do not, like other animals, become wiser as they grow older; they merely become more skilled at defending their own fictions. Moreover, the way they interpret the world often perpetuates the early pain and hurt so often associated with family interaction. The complaints reported to therapists frequently contain some version of "My mother never loved me," or "My father never thought I was worth much." Whether these reports are factual or simply a faulty interpretation reinforced by many tellings can usually never be known.

This process of creating and defending a story clearly emerges in much marriage counseling, where a single happening may be used by both husband and wife as "evidence" for their different conclusions. Consider, for example, this case of Jack and Jill (from Laing, Phillipson, & Lee, 1966):

> Jack and Jill are ostensibly in love and each feels he or she loves the other, but Jack is not sure whether Jill loves Jack, and Jill is not sure whether Jack loves Jill ....Suppose that Jack ... persistently refuses to infer from Jill's behavior toward him, however loving, that she "really" loves him, but believes, despite evidence from Jill's manifest behavior ... that she loves Tom, Dick, or Harry. A curious feature of Jack's tendency to attribute to Jill a lack of love for him and a love for Tom, Dick, or Harry ... often seems to be that he

> tends to make this attribution in inverse proportion to
> Jill's testimony and actions to the contrary ... Jack may
> reason: "Look at all the things that Jill is doing to try to
> prove to me that she loves me. If she really loved me she
> would not have to be so obvious about it and try so
> hard ... .She must be trying to cover up her true feelings.
> She probably loves Tom." (p. 24)

As the authors noted, Jack has clearly created a story that is
untenable for Jill, in that whatever she says or does will only
serve as further "proof" for Jack's suspicions.

Similarly, it is not unusual for a child in a family to be
placed in this kind of untenable position when other family
members create a story about him or her and defend their
story in the face of contrary evidence. The following is from a
clinical report as reviewed by Vogel and Bell (1967):

> ... in one family which was very concerned with the
> problems of achievement, the focus of the family's prob-
> lems was the eldest son. Although he was receiving passing
> grades in school ... the parents were very critical of his
> school performance. Because of this pressure, the child
> worked hard and was able to get somewhat better marks on
> the next report card. However, the mother stoutly main-
> tained that her son didn't deserve those grades, that he
> must have cheated, and she continued to criticize him for
> his school performance. (p. 431)

Viewed in this way, communication is always a process of
stirring up meanings (images, ideas, and feelings) in the other
person by getting that person to recall something already
known, felt, or believed. Weaver and Ness (1957) make a
similar point:

> Thus it comes about that no one ever can really tell another
> person a story; the best that the storyteller can hope for is
> that the communicatee may be stimulated into telling
> himself a story of the sort that the communicator wants
> him to hear. As speakers, the best that we can do is to use
> audible and/or visible symbols which may touch off in our
> listeners certain elements of their past experiences; this we
> try to do in such a manner that the listeners will produce

for themselves the meaningful patterns which we want them to have. (p. 10–11)

By way of summary, this chapter has presented some views from anthropology, linguistics, semantics, and family therapy. We have seen that although human communication is sometimes defined solely in terms of symbolic response, this is not altogether accurate because humankind has not abandoned the animal capacity to use and respond to signs. Rather, it has overlaid that capacity with a peculiar talent for using and manipulating symbols, thus creating an elaborate fabric of interwoven meaning—part signification, part symbolization. With the talent for using symbols, human beings create stories and models—world models, family models, and personal models. In other words, one comes to "know" what the world is like, what one's family is like, and what oneself is like. One then perceives world, family and self through the screen of models, and reacts to his/her own misperceptions as though they were ultimate truths.

The propensity of humans for creating stories and then defending their creations is associated with several forms of seriously disturbed family behavior: the scapegoating of a child, the support of often-outrageous family myths, and of pathological "pseudomutuality." These will be considered further in Chapter 7.

Chapter 1 looked at the family as a system; this chapter has explored the feature of family life which, more than any other, links the family into a system—its communication. We have seen that human communication somehow works, although it is imperfect at best, and we have considered some of the weaknesses arising out of its very nature. We have seen how meaning is made out of raw sensory data through a process of interpretation, or decoding, and how the manipulation of symbols enables us to make our own meaning from minimal cues. We have also mentioned some of the many sources of communication "breakdown" at both technical and semantic levels, often involving error in signification as well as error or distortion in symbolic interpretation.

In the next chapter we will see how meaning is made at two

levels: the communicative and the metacommunicative levels (where we communicate *about* communication or about the relationship between communicants). We will also review Watzlawick, Beavin, and Jackson's axioms of communication, having to do with continuousness of communication, content and relationship features, and problems of "punctuation."

Levels of Meaning: Messages and Metamessages

DEFINING A MESSAGE

A message consists of whatever unit of behavior serves to link the parties of communication (Mortensen, 1972, p. 19). As we have seen, messages may be verbal or nonverbal, intentional or unintentional, sign-based or symbol-based, real or imagined, human or non-human. We have said, too, that to qualify as a message, a unit of behavior must be interpreted in some way, occur in some context, and be capable of eliciting a response. Beyond these points of general agreement, there are many variations in the way messages can be classified. In this chapter we will look at classification based on levels of meaning, that is, messages and metamessages.

DEFINING A METAMESSAGE

In its simplest definition, metacommunication refers to any communication *about* a communication (Ruesch & Bateson, 1951, p. 209). More precisely, a metamessage means any message having to do with (1) another message, or (2) the relationship between communicators. Because the metacommunicative level is crucial to the way a family makes meaning together, we shall look more closely at these two functions. Remembering that some communication is always occurring, whether intentional or not, we should add that *meta*communication, too, is always occurring, since every message contains implications about the relationship and about how the message is to be taken.

A Metamessage That Comments About the Message

First, the metamessage serves the purpose of letting the other person know how to interpret the message. It can reinforce the message, change it, or even contradict it. As Bateson (1972) noted, all communication can be magically modified by the accompanying metacommunication (p. 178). This kind of message-about-a-message can be spoken, as when a sergeant barks, "That's an order, soldier!"—or the reverse, "I'm only kidding," or "Please don't take me seriously." However, the metamessage is far more likely to be expressed or implied in modalities that *parallel* the spoken word. For instance, a mother may quiet a noisy child in church by saying "Sssh," frowning, and placing her finger on her lips, while touching the child with her other hand in a quieting gesture. Here the "Sssh" message is *complemented* by her gesture and her facial expression. Together her behaviors combine to provide *redundancy* for her message and to make it clear to the child that she means for her message to be taken seriously. Quite a different effect would have been created had she giggled while "Ssh-ing" him, because children are quick to understand the metamessage, "This is a game." Jules Henry (1973) provides an instance from his work as a live-in family therapist, when a serious message was misinterpreted as play by a 17-month-old girl on the basis of her mother's meta-communicative cues. In this case, the mistake was almost fatal:

> On the second day Mrs. Jones and I were talking on the front porch steps and Harriet (17 months old) was playing nearby. Harriet would run all the way down to the edge of the walk heading toward the road, and Mrs. Jones would go running after her in a jolly way and catch her just before she out into the road, and the baby would laugh joyously. Harriet took this as a game, and Mrs. Jones went running after her two or three times to prevent the baby from running into the road....When our backs were turned for a moment Harriet got out almost to the middle of the road, and a huge oil truck came tearing around the corner and missed the baby by about ten feet. We then went back to the porch, and the chasing game between Harriet and her mother developed again. (p. 34)

In this account, the message "stay out of the street" was not taken as a serious injunction, because it was negated by the stronger metamessage that the whole thing was a game.

Not all cases of incongruity between message and meta-message are dangerous or even undesirable—in fact, it is the basis of all play and much of our humor. Bateson, in an early formulation of the concept of metacommunication (1955), noted that all animals go through the motions of fighting or making threats toward one another, while at the same time making it clear that "this is play" (pp. 39–50). Such behavior can also be observed in the social behavior of small children who spend a good part of their waking activities engaged in bluff, playful threat, and various forms of teasing.

Interpersonal trouble growing out of metacommunication often occurs in a family when a *loving* verbal message is accompanied by an unloving nonverbal metamessage of rejection, since the nonverbal metamessage is usually more believable, particularly if the receiver is a very young child. Here the speaker's tone of voice and body language carry considerably more weight than do the words, and this is of profound significance in family interaction. The wife who speaks seductive words to her husband, but stiffens and withdraws from an intimate advance, or the mother who calls her child to her with kindly words, but in an icy, threatening tone, are both familiar figures to the family therapist. In both instances, verbal messages are incongruent with the accompanying nonverbal metamessage, and the receiver must decide whether to act on the words or on the other cues from the speaker. A potentially more serious aspect of this matter will come up again in Chapter 13, when we consider the nature of paradox and the "double-bind" hypothesis of schizophrenia.

A Metamessage That Comments About the Relationship

Relational metamessages are inherent in every verbal or nonverbal message because each implies the speaker's conviction that he or she has the *right* to address that particular message to that particular person. Beyond this, relational metamessages can reflect the status of the speakers, similarities and differences in speakers, power-powerlessness in the relationship, or a simple recognition or registration of the other's attempt to communicate.

Metamessages about relationship seem to take on greater significance in families where problems already exist. As Watzlawick, et al. (1967) noted, the more spontaneous and healthy a relationship, the more the relationship aspects recede into the background. "Conversely," they wrote, "'sick' relationships are characterized by a constant struggle about the nature of the relationship, with the content aspect of communication becoming less and less important" (p. 48).

To even acknowledge another person's attempt to communicate (whether the acknowledgement is positive or negative, in agreement or disagreement) always evokes the metamessage, "We are communicating." The total absence of acknowledgement may contain any or all of a lengthy assortment of hurtful relational metamessages: "We are *not* communicating," "I do not wish to relate to you," "You are not worth my attention," or even the lethal metamessage "You do not exist," to mention only a few possibilities. Perhaps more than any other kind of emotional trauma, adults in therapy tend to recall instances of this kind, when their childhood attempts to get through to a parent were ignored, rebuffed, or discounted. The metamessage about a child's personal significance may never be forgotten by the child, and may well be incorporated into his or her self-view as an adult. This will come up again in Chapter 13, when we consider confirming and disconfirming response forms in family interaction.

Relational metamessages may be spoken directly, of course ("Who do you think you are to speak to me that way?" or "How dare you talk that way to your mother!"), but are more often hidden within some other verbal content, as when two persons habitually argue about irrelevant issues simply to establish who is superior (Watzlawick, et al., 1967, pp. 34–43). Repeated family fights may express the metamessage, "We can't get along," and members may strive to live up to the implied relationship, no matter what the topic of discussion. Analysis of long-term interaction in a family will usually disclose metacommunicative evidence of family coalitions or splits, such as "Dad always sides with Jimmie in an argument," "You always take her side!" or "Mom and Sis always fight." (These repeated patterns of interaction can also be interpreted as *rules* of the family system.)

In the case of a couple whose marriage has turned into a chronic struggle for supremacy, the metamessage "We always fight" become considerably more significant than the various topics about which they fight. Any subject, even their love for each other, can serve as openers for a fight, as this satirical bit of dialogue illustrates (Ciardi, 1967):

"I love you" she said.
"I adore you" he said.
"I love you more" she said.
"More than what?" he said.
"Than you love me" she said.
"Impossible" he said.
"Don't argue" she said.
"I was only . . ." he said.
"Shut up" she said. (p. 7)

Briefly summarizing the subject of metacommunication: a

metamessage is a message *about* a message. It performs two possible functions: it comments about the message, usually indicating how the message is intended or should be interpreted, and it also comments about the nature of the relationship between the communicators. A metamessage may be expressed directly in words, or it may be expressed indirectly but still in words, so that the metamessage is imbedded in some other spoken content. A metamessage may also be expressed through some nonverbal means, such as a gesture, facial expression, body position, touch, distance from or closeness to the other person. (Consider, for instance, the raised eyebrow of disbelief, the sneer of superiority, the sigh of resignation—all these are powerful comments about how the relationship is perceived perhaps more powerful than any words.) Because each modality has significance for others, we can picture two persons in one another's presence as continuously sending and receiving multiple simultaneous messages, which may or may not be congruent with one another.

AXIOMS OF COMMUNICATION

Much of what we have been saying in this chapter has been formalized by Watzlawick, Beavin, and Jackson (1967) in a set of axioms having to do with human communication and metacommunication. Although originally published as "tentative axioms," these have proved basic to the study of human interaction and are especially relevant to a systems view of family communication. Three of these axioms are summarized below. (Other axioms will be discussed in Chapter 8).

Axiom #1. One cannot not communicate. Just as behavior has no opposite, so communication has no opposite. Communication takes place whether it is intentional, conscious, or successful. The message sent may not always be the message received, but *some* message is continually being evoked in the mind of the receiver. We do not, of course, speak constantly, so the verbal mode is termed *discontinuous*; however, communication is itself *continuous* because some sort of nonverbal behavior is always going on, and because the absence of speech—silence—has strong message import.

Family members are not always aware of the effect of their silence on others; in fact, an habitually silent member often behaves *as if* he or she could avoid communicating by remaining silent, appearing not to realize that silence is always interpreted in some way by others, in the same way that speech is interpreted. As already noted, children are especially vulnerable to rebuffs in the form of parental withdrawal, because a child is quick to interpret a parent's unresponsiveness as meaning that s/he, the child, is un-important, bad, or otherwise undeserving of adult attention.

This subjective interpretation of silence also play a signif-icant part in marital communication. A frequent complaint of wives—possibly the most frequent—is that their husbands don't talk to them enough. The plea, "Talk to me, Harold" (Fast, 1971, p. 26), seems to express a widely felt emotional void in the lives of wives in our culture. To illustrate this point, sociologist Mirra Komarovsky (1966), in gathering material about the "blue-collar marriage," noted a prevalent view, as expressed in the following excerpt from an interview with a 36-year-old husband:

> One thing that gets my wife is that I don't talk enough. She wants to sit down and talk. And there is nothing to talk about. I have been married to her for thirteen years and I am talked out. I can't find anything to talk about. The kind of things that she wants to talk about are kids' stuff and trivial, like Mrs. X had her tooth pulled out. I'd rather work around the house or work on the car. (p. 150)

A number of explanations for silence in the marital context have been advanced. It may be evidence of cultural differences between men and women, as in the above statement, which Komarovsky sees as evidence of a "trained incapacity to share"; it may reflect a general impoverishment of both working and home environments (there really may be little to talk *about*); it may be a consequence of the belief of many adult males that expressing feelings is unmanly and that a wife should not be "bothered" with a man's problems. It may even have a deep-seated psychoanalytic explanation, such as that advanced by Leslie Farber (1972), who suggested that all real talk between a man and a woman is perceived by the male as sexually provocative. Thus, once a couple has agreed on an ongoing sexual relationship, the male sees no further need for talk except for the exchange of necessary reports or requests ("Pass the salt").

Whatever the explanation for these silent partners, there is some evidence that the wife of a noncommunicative husband is more likely to interpret his silence as *disinterest in her* than to accept any of the other possible reasons. As the wife in the Komarovsky sees as growing out of a "trained incapacity to day, what has she got? Just the children and what the neighbors have said or done" (p. 150). This feeling of inadequacy on the part of women was also evident in a study by McCrosky, Larson, & Knapp (1971), in which wives were asked to describe the typical patterns of interaction with their husbands. From a range of alternative choices the pattern that the wives in this study *most frequently* attributed to their husband was one in which the husbands were perceived by their wives as not really interested in them, as relatively unresponsive, and relatively unconcerned about their wives' interests and activities (p. 172). For these wives at least, the metamessage "You do not interest me" had taken precedence over all others.

At a more deeply pathological level, Watzlawick, et al. (1967) hypothesized that the attempt not to communicate is part of the schizophrenic "dilemma," adding, "Since any communication ... implies commitment and therely defines the sender's view of his relationship with the receiver, it can be hypothesized that the schizophrenic behaves as if he would avoid commitment by not communicating" (p. 51). It can also be supposed that the attempt not to communicate, on the part of normal family members, might serve a similar purpose by denying responsibility for the relationship. Thus the metamessages of silence might be, "I am indifferent to you," "You are not worth my attention," or "We are not relating." At any rate, *some* message is always evoked by silence—usually a painful one.

Axiom #2. Every communication has a content and a relationship aspect, such that the latter classifies the former and is therefore a metacommunication. With a basic under-standing of the nature of metacommunication, it is now possible to review this axiom, which provides another way of looking at levels of meaning.

In an early work (Ruesch & Bateson, 1951), Bateson described the dual function of each bit of communication as being both a *report* and a *command.* This distinction re-sembles the operation of a computer, which needs two kinds of input in order to function. First, it needs data and, second, it needs instructions about what to do with the data. Bateson further explained these two aspects:

> Whatever communication we consider . . . it is evident that every message in transit has two sorts of "meaning." On the one hand, the message is a statement or report about events at a previous moment, and on the other hand it is a command—a cause or stimulus for events at a later moment. Consider the case of three neurons, A, B, and C, in a series, so that the firing of A leads to the firing of B, and the firing of B leads to the firing of C. Even in this extremely simple case, the message transmitted by B has the two sorts of meaning referred to above. On the one hand it can be regarded as a "report" to the effect that A fired at a previous moment; and on the other hand it is a "command" or cause for C's later firing. (pp. 179–180)

A similar sort of sequential action seems to occur whenever one person speaks with another. The words convey some information the speaker has, and those words are also the basis for the receiver's subsequent action. So whenever a person speaks, he or she is not only making a statement, but is also trying to get the receiver to respond in some particular way, to do something or to believe something.

The report aspect of a message conveys information and is, therefore, synonymous in human communication with the *content* of the message. The command aspect, on the other hand, refers to what sort of message it is, how it is to be taken, or to the relationship between the communicants (Watzlawick, et al., 1967, p. 52).

The literal content of a message (the report) appears to be its least troublesome aspect in family interaction. Mutual understanding at this level requires only that both parties share a common language, that the signal is reasonably ungarbled, and that both parties interpret the words in a similar way. It is not uncommon, however, to find misunderstandings even at this level, usually because of cross-generational vocabulary differences, such as teen slang. The results of this sort of misunderstanding are not usually serious and may sometimes be more humorous than painful. Most adults can recall with amusement some occasion when, as children, they misinterpreted adult conversations, as, for example, when the term "guerilla warfare" evoked an image of apes swinging through the trees; or as in Edgar Dale's account (1971), when the little boy ended the Pledge of Allegiance by calling for "liver, tea, and just fish for all" (p. 189).

Confusion about the report aspect of a message is not always so innocent, however, sometimes the use of inappropriate words to a child is evidence of a more serious family problem of fantasy-based relations. Thus talk may seem to be addressed, not to a real person present, but to some "phantom construction" of the speaker. Jules Henry's (1973) account of the interaction between a father and his seven-year-old son addresses this point:

> Last night at supper, when Bobby and his father got into some sort of an argument, the father said, "That's *a posteriori*, Bobby."
>
> Such language puts the father out of reach; perhaps it makes him possessed of a mysterious lingo, quite beyond the child's powers of comprehension. For Bobby to understand him he would have to be well on in college, but he is only a seven-year-old. Since Dr. Jones [the father] is communicating with a somebody who isn't there, a somebody who cannot decode the signals he is sending, let us call this *phantom communication*. (p. 80)

This problem of relating to phantoms, fantasies, and fictions instead of to real people will be considered further in Chapter 6.

Both report and command elements of an utterance may

be verbal and explicit, as "I'm cold (*report*); close the window (*command*)." It may be, however, that the report is spoken but the command is only implied, hence subject to more than one interpretation. If a speaker simply says, "I'm cold," the report aspect of his message will probably be clear to any English-speaking person, but several possible commands may be inferred. The listener may think he is being blamed for the other's discomfort and so reacts defensively ("Well, I do the best I can to keep this drafty old house warm . . . "); he or she may interpret the message as an order for him/her to take some action to make the speaker more comfortable, and will then react with resentment at being ordered around ("Go get your own sweater!" or "Why don't *you* go down and see about the furnace for a change?") In either event, if the receiver believes the speaker wishes him to do something about the coldness, he will respond in some way to the implied command as well as to the simple report.

It is also possible that the receiver "hears" only the report element of a message and misses the implied command entirely, and so responds only to the report. In families, unspoken commands are a common source of hurt and resentment because one member failed to act in response to what the other had in mind, *but did not say*. The curious thing about this kind of message-sender is that he or she generally expects others to know about his or her needs without being told—in fact, may believe that the other *has* been told. The husband who asks in an irritated tone, "When's dinner?" may believe that he has adequately informed his wife that he is hungry and in a hurry to eat; the mother who has cheerfully told her teenage daughter to "go on out and have a good time," may secretly feel hurt when the daughter does just that. Mother may later report to a friend (or therapist) that daughter "ought to have known" that her mother needed help with the dishes. So the wife who feels depressed but smiles bravely and says, "I'm just fine; don't worry a bit about me," may feel even more depressed and rejected if her husband takes her "report" literally and misses the implied "command"—an appeal for his support and reassurance—feeling that he too "should have known." In much the same way, a couple's sexual dysfunction often persists for the life of a marriage simply because neither can produce a clearly stated message about what pleases or displeases. The explanation is usually the same: "He (she) should have known."

In addition to unspoken command messages, other kinds of latent messages are often embedded in the manifest content of a spoken message. All messages require some decoding; some need more translating than others, notably those relating to wants or needs that the speaker does not wish to reveal directly. For example, people for a variety of reasons, may feel embarrassed or self-conscious about sending direct messages concerning their feelings. Instead, they create verbalizations that only minimally resemble their internal experience. We have already seen the person who expects others to know his or her needs without being told— the person who withholds vital information, but is hurt when others do not do as desired. To this we should add the disguised-need message sender—that person who initiates a discussion quite apart from the real issue. Often, for instance, a child's academic-sounding question conceals a personal fear that he does not choose to reveal directly. ("Do bad men ever run off with little boys?") Even a four-year-old boy, already conditioned by the culture in "manliness" will be aware that his question, "Will the doggy bite?", in the presence of a large dog, is somehow more acceptable than the truth of the matter: "I'm afraid the doggy will bite me."

The marriage or family counselor is well aware of this disguised-need phenomenon, recognizing that the concerns first mentioned by their clients in a therapy or counseling session are usually not the real concerns that brought them to therapy. Only later, as the clients become more comfortable, are the false "problems" dropped in favor of the real ones.

Things communicative are not always what they appear, and it is well to recognize that the command element of a message may not have the syntax of command. As we have seen, it may sound like a simple report of fact to everyone but the speaker, who alone knows what he/she means or wants. Another variation is the command that takes the form of a question. Almost any native speaker of English will recognize that utterances that begin with "*Why* do you *always* do that?" or "*Must* you do that ... ?" are not really questions that require answers so much as commands to desist or take some kind of remedial action. Also, such exchanges as:

Child: Can I have a piece of candy?
Mother: You don't want to ruin your teeth, do you?

form a request-denial sequence, although the mother's refusal is phrased as a question. An older child would very likely recognize the mother's response as a denial of the request (and a command to leave the candy alone), but a younger child might find her question completely irrelevant. If he then proceeded to eat the candy, his punishment for "disobeying mother" might appear both unfair and undeserved to him because he had missed the command aspect embedded in her response.

Axiom #3. The nature of a relationship is contingent upon the punctuation of the communicational sequences between the communicants. In Chapter 1, when speaking of the transactional perspective, we discussed how many family problems arise out of uncertainly about what is stimulus and what is response—where the sequence of events is perceived differently by different participants. As an example, Watzlawick, et al. (1967) cite the case of the "nagging" wife and her "passive" husband. The wife claims, "I only nag because you withdraw," and the husband retorts that, "I only withdraw because you nag," each believing the other starts their fights. This axiom emphasizes the circularity of every communicative sequence, in which there is no true starting place and no end—no stimulus and no response. To an observer, it would appear that a sequence of communicative events is an uninterrupted flow; to the participants, however, it is likely to seem that the flow is broken up into stimulus-response units, so that one party sees the other as a stimulus and himself/herself as simply a responder, whereas the other sees the opposite sequence: he/she is only a responder/reactor, and the other *started the trouble*. By punctuation, the authors mean the breaking up of a transactional pattern into smaller sequences that have their own beginnings and endings. The human tendency to create such sequential patternings has a good deal of significance in families where either continuing conflict or pathology develops, as Watzlawick and Beavin (1977) noted:

> Discrepancies in the punctuation of jointly experienced events are in fact at the root of many conflicts in most areas of human interaction, and the ever present blindness for the other's punctuation, coupled with the naive conviction that reality is the way *I* see (punctuate) these events, almost invariably leads to the mutual charges of badness or madness. (p. 65)

Summary of "The Communication Perspective"

Family communication differs from other human communication only in its emotional intensity. Because of the intimate nature of the relationships involved, any miscommunication in the family is likely to be more painful and the consequences more serious than in other human groups. Nevertheless, the same principles apply as elsewhere.

Chapter 3 treated the making of meaning, and we saw that human communication, although imperfect, somehow seems to work. Breakdowns do occur, however, both at the technical level and—more likely—at the semantic level. Thus, even though *some* meaning is always being made, the message sent is seldom the message received. Chapter 4 examined the various levels of meaning—communicative and metacommunicative, and reviewed three axioms of communication: we cannot *not* communicate, communication has both content and relationship features, and problems often occur as a result of failure of communicants to recognize differences in the "punctuation" of interaction.

Throughout Part II, it has been emphasized that each individual is selective in screening inputs, and that even those inputs that are permitted into conscious awareness are subjectively interpreted in light of the person's prior beliefs, private fantasies, needs and illusions. However, this suggestion of *intra*personal causality is far from a complete explanation, and we need to take a more transactional view in order to understand family communication. This will be the focus of Part V, in which we consider response styles in families.

The next chapter, Chapter 5, begins the study of relationships in the family, which grow out of communication, but also serve to influence communication—a transactional pattern with which we are by now familiar.

REFERENCES

Barnlund, D. C. (1962). Toward a meaning-centered philosophy of communication. *Journal of Communication, 11*, 198–202.

Barnlund, D. C. (1970). A transactional model of communication. In Sereno, K. K., & Mortensen, D. C., *Foundations of Communication Theory*, pp. 83–102. New York: Harper.

Bateson, G. (1955). A theory of play and fantasy. *APA Psychiatric Report, 2*, 39–50.

Bateson, G. (1972). *Steps to an Ecology of Mind*. New York: Ballantine.

Brown, C. T., & Keller, P. W. (1973). *Monologue to Dialogue: An Exploration of Interpersonal Communication*. Englewood Cliffs, N. J.: Prentice-Hall.

Cherry, C. (1961). *On Human Communication*. New York: Science Editions.

Ciardi, J. (1967). Manner of speaking, *Saturday Review*, December 23, p. 7.

Dale, E. (1971). Clear only when known. In Devito, J. A. (Ed.), *Communication: Concepts and Processes*, pp. 189–194. Englewood Cliffs, N. J.: Prentice-Hall.

Drucker, P. F. (1957, August). The new philosophy comes to life, *Harper's Magazine*, p. 36.

fusion. (See, for instance, Bowen's "undifferentiated family ego mass" or Minuchin's "enmeshed family" in Part IV). It can occur in the case of a marital dyad or can encompass an entire family.

In the case of merged marital partners, the two adopt a clinging, possessive attitude, implying, "I am nothing without you." Each tends to disregard the other's autonomy, finishing the other's sentences, expressing the other's "real" feelings, or trying to provoke predictible, cliché-like responses from the other. Communication between them may take the form of endless efforts of one partner to make the other feel or appear responsible for him or her—failures, disappointments, or unfilled needs.

The state of merger between two persons is especially evident if one partner is lost through death or separation. Not only does the remaining partner experience a normal feeling of loss and grief, but may also feel that he or she is personally disintegrating because his or her own sense of self was fused with the lost partner.

In a merger between parent and child, the major threat to their system is the growth of the child, which a parent, often in collusion with the entire family, may strive mightily to prevent. If an adolescent's efforts to free himself or herself from a family merger continue to fail, he or she may fall back into a lasting dependency, symbiosis, or even psychosis.

Whole families may join in a merger, in which case the possibility of one member withdrawing can threaten the entire system to such an extent that the family unites against the member's efforts to extricate himself, denying his right and need to be autonomous. Laing's (1965a) account of the case of "Joan" includes this description of a girl's own feelings in just such a circumstance:

> My doctors just tried to make me a "good girl" and patch things up between me and my parents. They tried to make me fit in with my parents. This was hopeless. They couldn't see that I was longing for new parents and a new life. None of the doctors seemed to take me seriously, to see how sick I was and what a big change I needed in life. No one seemed to realize that if I went back to my family I would be sucked back and lose myself. It would be like the photograph of a

big family group taken from far away. You can see that
there are people there but you can't be sure who is who. I
would just be lost in a group. (p. 173)

It has been postulated that every transaction between
persons has two components: a *subject* (one who acts) and an
object (one who is acted upon). Put another way, the subject
provokes a response and the object responds; the subject is
autonomous and the object is dependent. The ways in which
these two functional components interact has been the theme
of much theorizing (see, for instance, Boszormenyi-Nagy &
Framo, 1965). In a merged family it is difficult to tell at any
given moment who is acting as subject and who as object
because the roles are blended. For example, because one
member knows the other's role response so well, the initiating
utterance of one member actually contains or at least sets up
the other's predictable response ("Isn't that right, dear?",
accompanied by "coaching" in the form of vigorous head-
nodding.)

The merged family is a relatively closed system in the sense
that there is a decided effort to remain always the same, to
resist change and avoid differences among members. This
may require denying that change has occurred or that
differences exist, carefully observing family taboos about
subjects that cannot be discussed, or by attempts to convince
a "deviant" member that he or she *ought* to accept the family
viewpoint on every matter. In such a family system, difference
is treated as disloyalty.

A merged family is also closed to outside intrusion, which
may threaten the family's togetherness by introducing new
and unpredictable data. To illustrate, a young husband
discovers that his new wife still owes her primary allegiance to
her family of origin, and on every issue between them must
"take on" her entire family or permit himself to be absorbed
into her amorphous family structure by accepting his assigned role (passive and compliant). Even a therapist who
attempts to treat such a family risks becoming part of the
merger.

RIGID ROLE RELATIONSHIPS

In some relationships the subject-object roles described earlier are clearly differentiated, but not reciprocal. That is, one person is identified as the continual object and is never permitted to be subject to another's object. Here the object-person is essentially at the whim of the other person's internal needs and accepts whatever role or responsive stance the other requires of him. He is always the complementary not-Self that is required to support the other's Self—but in the process, his own Self is never permitted to develop. Thus the person who is a perpetual object cannot act to fill his own needs, but is always used to fill the other's ego needs. As he becomes more and more involved in being an object, freedom to choose a role response is lost and growth potential is drastically reduced.

It is not uncommon for a child to be force-fed an object role opposite a parent's subject role, in which case the child can respond but can never initiate. Even his or her response must be in the prescribed direction. If the child rebels against the assigned object role, the relationship may then regress to the "internal dialogue" form, in which the child's real behavior is disregarded and he/she is treated *as if* the role were being performed in accordance with expectations.

Behavioral devices through which one person binds another into an object role are varied. Children are especially vulnerable to the pressure of parental needs, whether spoken or unspoken, conscious or unconscious. To illustrate, parents who are irresponsible and childlike themselves may serve to bind a child into responsible parent-like behavior long before the child is emotionally equipped for an adult role; constantly fighting parents may encourage their child to adopt a judge-like or placator object role, or the child of disturbed, unhappy, or suicidal parents may attempt to assume responsibility for "straightening out" the parents or saving their marriage. If a child's efforts fail, as they usually do, the child may then, perhaps unconsciously, assume guilt for the unhappiness, desertion, or even death of a parent.

Nowhere is a family's "system" aspect more evident than in this matter of subject-object role complementarity, where we see clear evidence of the control that a system can impose on its members. Complementarity of roles is essential for equilibrium of the family system; however, the process of maintaining such equilibrium in a dysfunctional family may be destructive for individual members, as we have already seen. Thus, whenever a member resists accepting a system-required complementary role, strong pressure may be exerted on him or her to behave in such a way as to restore homeostatic balance to the system. Restoration of balance is a complex process which may involve coercing, coaxing, masking, and many other devices (Spiegel, 1957). The pressure to restore family homeostatic balance is unwitting and largely unconscious on the parts of the members involved, as Spiegel noted:

> A constant observer of the family...has a somewhat contrary impression that much of what occurs in the way of behavior is not under the control of any one person or even a set of persons, but is rather the upshot of complicated processes beyond the ken of anyone involved. Something in the group process itself takes over as a steering mechanism and brings about results which no one anticipates or wants. (p. 1)

Part III has reviewed the human needs for both connection and autonomy, stressing the fact that both are crucial for individual health. Relatedness is essential, but without a sense of personal autonomy, relationships can be fearful and sometimes overwhelming. In Chapter 6, we have considered several sorts of dysfunctional family relationships that interfere with either the need for relatedness or the need for autonomy: dehumanizing relations, sham relations, merged relations, and rigid role relations. Chapter 7 will explore some of the more pathogenic relations frequently found in seriously disturbed families.

Pathogenic Relational Patterns in Severely Disturbed Family Systems

Although the relational patterns just discussed (dehumanization, sham, merger, and rigid role relations) have the potential of becoming severe enough to be termed pathological, they also occur to a lesser degree in many families identified as normal. There are, however, certain kinds of relationships that by their very nature are associated with family pathology. In this chapter, six of these relational patterns will be considered: pseudomutuality, mystification, the over-protective mother and inadequate father combination, marital schism and marital skew, perverse triangles, and the phenomenon of the family scapegoat. Although these patterns have been observed and reported as occurring in a very literal way in some families, it should be emphasized that these are theoretical formulations developed as hypothetical constructs and presented in an exaggerated way to explain complex phenomena of family interaction.

PSEUDOMUTUALITY AND FAMILY MYTH

A disordered kind of family relating has been described by the research team headed by Lyman Wynne, of the National Institute of Mental Health (Wynne, Ryckoff, Day, & Hirsch, 1958). Identified as "pseudomutuality," this form of family relating is based on sham and represents a disturbed pathological solution to the separateness-connectedness dilemma described in Chapter 5. First, the Wynne group identified three possible solutions to the problem of achieving both relatedness and individual identity. These are: mutuality, non-mutuality, and pseudomutuality. *Mutuality* is a general term describing a kind of relatedness that thrives on difference and tolerates diversion among its members. It is described as being best able to satisfy members' strivings for both relational complementarity *and* personal identity. *Non-mutuality* is a functional, role-related relationship which may be completely effective in getting a particular job done (as, for example, a sales clerk and a customer transacting business), but does not encourage or permit intimacy. In a family, non-mutuality may be as simple as "Wash you hands," or as complex as rearing a family together, but characteristically focuses attention on a third thing or event in the environment. It does not fill the need for intimacy, and may, in fact, be used as a defense against intimacy, for example, when a father converses freely with his adolescent son about sports or about a project in which they are both engaged, but withdraws and becomes uncomfortable if the son tries to discuss with him a sexual problem, returning the conversation to baseball as hurriedly as possible. *Pseudomutuality* refers to a quality of relating that creates a sense of intimacy, but is not genuine. The false sense of relatedness is achieved at the expense of personal growth and identity of members. The pseudomutual family is perceived as a closed system with a continuous boundary having no observable openings. It is a totally self-contained social system that is threatened by the intrusion of information from outside the system. (You may recognize this description as very much like the state of "merger" discussed earlier). A family may, over the years, build various shared mechanisms for maintaining its pseudomutuality, all of which serve the general function of retaining the family's *status quo* by restricting the growth and change of its members.

One such mechanism, according to Wynne, et al. (1958), is the *family myth*. This is not simply a deliberately false front erected by the family to deceive the public, but a genuine belief that is part of an inner image held by each member of the family. As we saw in the case of the mother who continued to insist that her husband was quite devoted to his family (although he had deserted them fifteen years earlier), the myth may go unchallenged despite its obvious untruth.

Several themes of family myth seem to be favored by pseudomutual families, as researchers have noted. One is the theme of *perpetual happiness and harmony,* which is possibly used by the family as a rationale for doing nothing about its problems. In one such family with a multitude of troubles, the mother insisted, and the father echoed:

> We are all peacefull ... .I like peace even if I have to kill someone to get it ... .A more normal, happy kid would be hard to find [of a son who was then in therapy]. I was pleased with my child! I was pleased with my husband! I was pleased with my life. I have always been pleased! I have had 25 years of the happiest married life ... .(Wynne, et al., 1958, p. 205)

Ferreira (1963) cited a family whose myth involved the father as a "happy man." No matter what happened, he wore a constant, wide, grotesque smile and said only cheerful, optimistic things, despite the obvious fact that things were not going at all well for the family. Because of their son's school problems, the family as a unit was prevailed upon to enter therapy, without much effect. About the case, Ferreira commented:

> After a few sessions of family therapy, it became quite apparent that this family did not show any inclination to face the many problems they had. Under the supposed

> leadership of the father, they spent most of the time smiling at each other . . . and staring at the therapist with fixed grins as if saying in a sort of nonverbal chorus, "See how happy we are." (p. 460)

Later, when the therapist provoked the father into momentarily dropping his smiling face mask, the whole family rushed to defend his "happiness." The family never returned for further therapy.

Another common theme of family myth is the "goodness" of the children—a bland, indiscriminate, but determined approval of anything any member of the family might do. Sometimes this expresses itself in terms of parental respect for self-determination and "freedom," but in practice it usually means that any corrective action is avoided and any violation of family rule, social standard, or even law is condoned. Thus, the murderous offspring may be described as a "happy child, never any trouble," and the pre-schizophrenic child may be described as being "obedient and considerate."

MYSTIFICATION

Karl Marx used the term "mystification" to mean *a plausible misrepresentation of what is going on or what is being done in the service of one socioeconomic class (the exploiters) against another class (the exploited)* (Laing, 1965b, p. 343). Laing employed Marx's term to describe a form of family pathology associated with evasion, denial, masking, or other misrepresentation, particularly having to do with how a family member *feels*. In many cases, the parents are the exploiters and a child the exploited. The dynamics appear similar to some dysfunctions already discussed, in that the exploiter seeks to induce confusion by attributing feelings to a person that that person does not experience. At the same time, mystification seeks to mask true feelings and thus to avoid authentic conflict. Although confused, the mystified person may not *feel* confused, and may be unaware of what is being done to him or her.

The function of mystification appears to be to maintain the status quo, and the mechanism is brought into play whenever a family member threatens the state of things as they are. It also functions to maintain rigid family roles and tries to force all members into pre-set role behaviors (Laing, 1965b). Laing explains this further by saying:

> The parents struggle to preserve their own interaction by maintaining their rigid preconceptions about who they are and who they ought to be, and the nature of the situation that characterizes family life. They are impervious to those emotional needs in their children that threaten to disrupt their preconceived schemata, and they mask or conceal disturbing situations in the family, acting as if they do not exist. (p. 351)

Mystification relies on sham in order to bring about the ultimate state of confusion. As we have seen, sham occurs in a less virulent form in many dysfunctional families, but Laing (1965b) illustrates parental sham in its most extreme form (mystification) in the following case of the psychiatric patient, "Ruby." In this case the family detested and despised the girl, an illegitimate child of the wife, but told her they loved her. When she began to suspect that they did not really care for her, she was told that she only imagined it or that she was being "paranoid." Thus the sham love presented to the girl (now 16 years old and pregnant) was combined with pressure on her to distrust her own experiencing. Laing continues with the case description:

> Like so many of our families, this one was haunted by the specter of scandal and gossip, by the fear of what "people" were saying or thinking, etc. When Ruby was pregnant, all this became intensified. Ruby thought "people were talking about her" (they in fact were) and her family knew they were, but when she told them about this, they tried to reassure her by telling her not to be silly, not to imagine things, that of course, no one was talking about her.
> This was just one of the many mystifications to which the girl was subjected. The following are a few of the others:
> (1) In her distracted, "paranoid" state, she said that she thought her mother, aunt, uncle, and cousin disliked her, picked on her, mocked her, despised her. As she got "well,"

she felt very remorseful about having thought such terrible things, and she said that her family had been "really good" to her and that she had a "lovely family."

Indeed, they gave her every reason to feel guilty for seeing them in this way, expressing dismay and horror that she should think that they did not love her.

In actuality, they told us [the therapists] that she was a slut and little better than a prostitute—and they told us this with vehemence and intensity. They tried to make her feel bad or mad for perceiving their real feelings.

(2) She guiltily suspected that they did not want her home from the hospital and accused them, in sudden outbursts, of wanting to get rid of her. They asked her how she could think such things, but in fact, they *were* extremely reluctant to have her at home.

They tried to make her think they wanted her home and to make her feel mad or bad if she perceived that they did not want her home, when, in fact, they did not want her home.

(3) Extraordinarily confused attitudes were brought into play when she became pregnant.

As soon as they could after hearing about it from Ruby, "mummy" and "mother" [her mother and her aunt] got her on the sitting-room divan, and while trying to pump hot soapy water into her uterus, told her with tears, reproaches, sympathy, pityingly and vindictively at once, what a fool she was, what a terrible plight she was in (just like her "mummy"), what a "bastard" the boy was ("just like her father"), what a disgrace, history was repeating itself, how could one expect anything else ...

This was the first time her true parentage had ever been explicitly made known to her.

(4) Subsequently, Ruby's feeling that people were talking about her began to develop in earnest. As we have noted, she was told that this was nonsense, and her family told us that everyone was "very kind" to her "considering ..."

(5) The whole family was choked with the sense of shame and scandal. While emphasizing this to Ruby again and again, they simultaneously told her that she was imagining things when she said that she thought people were talking about her.

(6) Her family *accused* her of being spoiled and pampered, but when she tried to reject their pampering, they told her (1) she was ungrateful, and (2) she needed them, she was still a child, etc., as though being spoiled was something *she* did ... According to the testimony of uncle, mother, and aunt to the researchers, this girl was repeat-

edly told by her uncle if she did not "mend her ways" she would have to get out of the house. We know that on two occasions she was actually told by him to go and she did. But when she said to him that he had told her to get out, *he denied it to her* (though not to us)!

Her uncle told us tremblingly how she had pawed him, run her hands over his trousers, how he was sickened by it. His wife said rather coolly that he did not give the impression of having been sickened at the time.

Ruby, when questioned later, had apparently no conscious idea that her uncle did not like being cuddled and petted. She thought he liked it, she had done it to please him.

Not just in one area, but in every conceiveable way—in respect of her clothes, her speech, her work, her friends—this girl was subject to mystification, permeating all the interstices of her being. (pp. 359–60)

When a person is told that she is happy, but does not *feel* happy, or when she expresses a feeling, but is told that s/he does *not* have such a feeling, then that person may become flooded with anxiety when personal experience differs from what others say the experience is. This may eventually create a weakening of her reality-testing capacity and she may begin to depend on others to interpret how she really feels. Thus, in a family context, the member may internalize the family sickness and have an active investment in maintaining the family's unhealthy state.

The seriousness of this type of family interaction cannot be overstated; as Laing (1965b) noted, "We have never yet seen a preschizophrenic who was not in a highly mystified state before his or her mainfest psychotic breakdown" (p. 360).

Because mystification is essentially communicative in nature and depends on *imperviousness* as a response form, it will be discussed further in Chapter 13, when we examine disconfirming responses.

THE OVERPROTECTIVE MOTHER AND INADEQUATE FATHER COMBINATION

David Levy (1943) noted more than forty years ago that maternal overprotectiveness is often associated with emotional disturbance in a child. It was not until 1948, however, that Frieda Fromm-Reichmann (1948) coined the term "schizophrenogenic mother" to describe a mother who, although not psychotic herself, related to her children in such a way that *they* tended to become emotionally disturbed. In addition to being overprotective, the schizophrenogenic mother was described as being aggressive, domineering, critical, and—above all—cold and unfeeling in her treatment of her child. Although the term "schizophrenogenic" has fallen into disuse, the destructive power of such a mother cannot be ignored in any discussion of family communication. The Palo Alto group for the Study of Schizophrenic Communication added to this basic description the quality of *incongruity* in a mother's behavior toward her child. The following ingredients, they reported, are frequently present in the family situation of a schizophrenic patient:

(1) A child whose mother becomes anxious and withdrawn if the child responds to her as a loving mother.

(2) A mother to whom feelings of anxiety and hostility toward her child are not acceptable, and who therefore denies these feelings while expressing overt loving behavior toward the child, implicitly encouraging his loving behavior toward her, from which she then withdraws.

(3) The absence of anyone in the family, such as a strong father, who can support the child in the face of the mother's contradictory behavior (Bateson, Jackson, Haley, & Weakland, 1956).

As the last item suggests, the effects of a mother's disturbed relationship with her child are felt most acutely when the father's personality is weak, ineffectual, or indifferent.

Even before publication of the germinal work by Bateson and his colleagues at Palo Alto, other characteristics of the *father* in disturbed families were noticed. In a long-term intensive study of family environment in which a schizophrenic grows up, Theodore Lidz and his associates at Yale University (Lidz, Cornelison, Fleck, & Terry, 1957) undertook one of the early research projects specifically involving the fathers of disturbed children. Based on their findings, the Lidz group identified four types of father, in terms of their style of relating to their families:

(1) The father who is in serious conflict with his wife. He is hostile to his wife, often seductive to his daughter(s), seeking to align the daughter(s) to his side against his wife.

(2) The father who is hostile toward his children, especially the sons. He is jealous and competitive with his sons and in constant rivalry with them for the wife's attention. Communication with his sons is usually limited to belittling them in various ways and undermining their self-confidence.

(3) The father who is grandiose and self-centered, demanding abject submission amounting almost to idolatry from his family. Although the children of such a father recognize their father's fantasy, they still support it.

(4) The father who sees himself as a failure, who is so preoccupied with his personal worthlessness that he is unable to relate adequately to either his wife or to his children.

It is significant that in all the cases observed by the Lidz group, the major disturbance created by one unstable parent could have been countered or relieved had the other parent been more stable. Only when *both* parents showed certain relational and communicative patterns, in combination, were the children seriously adversely affected. Specifically, these researchers concluded that when a cruel, sadistic father is teamed up with a passive, but emotionally overprotective mother, or when a weak, ineffectual father is combined with a cold, dominant, critical mother, the child is almost certain to suffer.

The Lidz group noted further that, in normal families, the relationship of each parent with a child could only be considered secondary to the marital relationship between parents. They reasoned that in less troubled families, a wife's emotional needs are met in large part by her husband. In marriages where this is not the case, a wife may turn to her child, form a pathogenic alliance with the child against the father, making impossible emotional demands upon the child which the child is not mature enough to fulfill. Haley's (1967) concept of "perverse triangles," discussed in the next section, adds to this formulation.

THE PERVERSE TRIANGLE

It cannot be emphasized too strongly that in a healthy family system, the husband-wife alliance is primary. When this relationship is disturbed, becomes secondary, or is non-existent (as in the case of Bowen's "emotional divorce"), a child is often drawn into an unhealthy coalition with a parent, forming what has been called a "perverse triangle" (Haley, 1967, pp. 16–21). Specifically this aspect of family pathology has the following characteristics:

(1) The people responding to each other in the triangle are not all peers; rather, one of them is of a different generation from the others.

(2) In the process of their interaction together, the person of one generation forms a coalition with a person of the other generation against his/her peer.

(3) The coalition between the two persons is denied. That is, there is certain behavior which indicates a coalition which, when it is queried, will be denied as a coalition. More formally, the behavior at one level that indicates there *is* a coalition is qualified by metacommunicative behavior indicating there is *not*.

In other words, the perverse triangle is one formed by three family members who are somehow breaching the separation between generations (Haley, 1967, p. 17).

By various other names, the perverse triangle appears in a goodly number of clinical descriptions of pathological families. We have just seen how Lidz and his colleagues analyzed it in their study of fathers. It also seems closely related to the psychoanalytic concept of the Oedipus conflict. When it involves a father in coalition with his son against the mother ("Women never do understand us men"), we have a situation described by Kiley (1983) as a prelude to the "Peter Pan syndrome," a pathology in which men try to remain little boys forever and avoid growing up. It figures in mother-in-law problems, where, for instance, the husband's mother may form an excessively intrusive coalition with her son against her son's wife. And it figures in any coalition formed between a grandparent and a member of either of the younger generations against a peer. Its most commonly noted and probably most pathogenic form is one we have already seen: where the "parentified" child, whose parents are in conflict, attempts to assume adult responsibility beyond his or her ability to handle, and the parents remain childlike, immature, and emotionally incompetent. A child burdened with such excessive relational demands, as a result, frequently becomes seriously disturbed.

MARITAL SCHISM AND MARITAL SKEW

The Lidz study of fathers was followed by a related project to examine various kinds of marital relationships that appeared to be associated with schizophrenia in the offspring (Lidz, et al., 1957). From these studies, two distinct relational patterns in marriage emerged and were identified as marital *schism* and marital *skew*. Each involves a peculiar form of intrafamilial communication believed to be pathogenic for the children. This project's findings repeated some of the team's earlier conclusions about fathers and provided further evidence to tie family relations to pathology in the children.

Marital Schism

One large group of marriages whose offspring became schizophrenic was marked by an absence of complementarity between partners, in that neither husband nor wife appeared able to support each other's needs. Interaction between partners was filled with open discord, in which each tried to coerce the other to conform with his or her own expectations, but was met by open or covert defiance, resulting in constant mutual recriminations. "Each spouse pursues his needs or objectives, largely ignoring the needs of the other, infuriating the partner and increasing ill-will and suspiciousness" (Lidz, et al., 1957, p. 243).

In such a schismatic marriage, each partner tends to undercut the other to the children and to compete for the children's favor. These are marriages marked by dislike and distrust, in which each partner more or less openly expresses fears that a child might resemble the other partner. Each parent attempts to instill his or her own values in the children, although these usually differ from the values of the spouse.

In the absence of support and affection from each other, there seems to be a tendency for each parent to turn to the child as a partner, casting the child into the role of surrogate mate and perhaps forming the perverse triangle that we have already seen. This places extreme burdens on the child, to which she/he may react in one of several possible ways:

(1) He might seek to widen the parental "gap," thus gaining one parent for himself and assuming the role of substitute lover.

(2) He might try to bridge the gap between his parents by devoting all his energies to them at the expense of his own ego development, or by offering himself as a scapegoat—an alternate target for the dissipation of parental rage and disappointment with each other.

(3) He might become immobilized, caught in the irreconcilable bind where love and loyalty for one parent would mean rejection by the other (Lidz, et al., 1957).

Marital Skew

A second distinctive relational pattern noted in the families of schizophrenic patients is that of marital skew. Lidz and his co-workers noted that these couples live together in a state of comparative harmony and even appear to fill each other's emotional needs in a way the schismatic relationship does not; but the marriages are distorted in that one partner (the dominant one) is seriously disturbed, and the disturbance is accepted as normal by the other partner. Thus the entire family's relationships appear to be organized around a central, dominating, figure, usually the mother, whose pathology comes to be accepted and perhaps shared by all (Lidz, et al., 1957, p. 243).

In the families in this group, the mother's psychosis is "masked" by the father, who allows her to dominate the family while he relinquishes all responsibility, becoming progressively weaker and more ineffectual as her illness becomes more pronounced. The following account from the Lidz study provides an example of such a skewed marriage (although it also has elements of a masked schism):

> The Swartz family was completely dominated by a paranoid mother who supported the family. Her husband had left her on one occasion, unable to tolerate her demands, but had returned long before the patient, the youngest son, had been born. Soon thereafter, the father suffered a nervous breakdown, after which he lived as a sort of handyman around the house and worked as a menial helper in the wife's business. The wife was extremely ambitious for her 4 sons, pushing them and dominating their lives, as well as making it clear that they must not become like their father. She was paranoidally fearful of outsiders, believing that their telephone was tapped and that the family was physically endangered because they were Jewish. A severe schism actually existed despite the peace between the marital couple. The mother was intensely protective of her oldest son, a gambler and embezzler, who consumed all of her attention as well as much of the family income. A chronic ambivalent conflict existed between them that tended to exclude the husband and the other sons. The husband did not intervene, but merely told his sons that the trouble in the family existed because they did not obey their mother as he did. (1957, p. 243)

In cases like this of a dominant pathological mother, Lidz found the *son* likely to develop a symbiotic bond with her, leading to his confusion of sexual identity, incestuous concerns, and a great assimilation of her disturbance. A daughter was less likely to be emotionally affected by her mother's pathology or by this type of pathogenic family system.

THE FAMILY WITH A SCAPEGOAT

As we have seen, if a person can get another family member to be crazy, then he or she can, for a time, disown his or her own craziness. By the same mechanism of projection whole families can sometimes forestall their own pathology by selecting and identifying a "crazy" child and using him or her as the family scapegoat.

The role of scapegoat is as old as recorded history; it is familiar to anthropologists and to historians of all primitive cultures as a device for drawing off evil influences from the rest of the tribe. The cultural belief has long prevailed that a group can achieve unity and safety by assigning to one member this role, in which he or she becomes the object of aggression and hostility for the entire group (Fraser, 1927). In recent years, psychiatric theorists have noted what appears to be the same phenomenon in troubled families, usually involving a disturbed or delinquent child. Vogel & Bell (1967), in particular, have explained the occurrence of scapegoating in a disturbed family by suggesting that when the family feels tension brought on by unresolved family conflicts (usually between husband and wife), the system requires some means for relieving the tension. When the tension becomes so severe that it cannot be contained without some kind of discharge, and *when the couple cannot confront one another directly in open communication*, their antagonisms may be turned against a relatively "safe" object, who then bears the brunt of all the family stress.

Scapegoating, perhaps more than any other relational pathology seen in families, can best be explained by viewing the family as a system. That is, repetitive patterns of interaction occur, not because of any one member's sickeness or internal conflicts, but because such a pattern is useful to the viability of the entire system. Each member's behavior is influenced by the state of the system at any given moment, and if a needed role is not played by one member, it must be played by another. Ackerman (1967) noted this kind of system interdependence in a family with a psychotic daughter:

> While treating a family with an only daughter—a girl of 16 years with an early and labile form of psychotic disorder—it struck me forcibly as I watched the family, and also as I viewed over and over the film record of these interviews, that when one part of the family came to life, the other part seemed to die. I am talking now of the sheer flow of affect, not words. The quality of coming to life, affectively speaking, seemed to swing back and forth, pendulum-fashion, from the parents to the daughter and back again. As I studied the process, it became plain that this was a consistent and repetitive pattern. If the young psychotic girl showed signs of life, the parents literally lay down and died before my eyes; if the parents became vocal and excited, the girl faded away. One part of the family seemed to draw the breath of life at the expense of the other. (p. 48)

The selection of a child to be the family scapegoat is largely an unconscious process, but seems to be based on certain characteristics of the child that mark him or her as different. These differences are not random, but have symbolic meaning that is related to the *real* source of tension in the family. For example, if the parents' unexpressed conflict involves the husband's lack of success, the child who is an underachiever in school may become the scapegoat because she/he symbolizes failure. (The father's "failure," of course, goes unmentioned.) Thus, the mother's criticism of her unsuccessful child may be an expression of her dissatisfaction with her husband's economic or occupational status—concerns that she will never express directly.

As we saw earlier, a child's sex or sibling position may be factors in selection as family scapegoat. If one or both parents had unpleasant experiences in their own family of origin with brothers, the scapegoat is likely to be one of their *male* children; if their early problems were with an older sibling, their current scapegoat may be their older child, and so on. In addition, a convenient victim for the scapegoat role may be found in the child with a low IQ, or a serious physical disease, or a striking abnormality such as a harelip or some other unattractive feature that allows the family to discriminate against him/her while rationalizing themselves as the victims: "What did we do to deserve such a child?"

Once selected as a scapegoat, the child is then expected to carry out his or her role as a "problem child," in order to continue to serve as a target for the release of family tension arising from other sources. The dynamics are simple: the child is "trained" to be exquisitely sensitive to arising tensions or anxieties, at which point she/he begins to act out in some fashion in order to direct attention to him/herself; the child attention and is yelled at or punished in some way, tension is relieved, and the system returns to normal. In terms of operant conditioning, negative reinforcement has occurred, in that the child's acting-out behavior serves to reduce the anxiety she/he feels when the system is out of balance. The child will repeat the behavior so long as it serves this purpose.

As we have already seen, a child is likely to internalize parental expectations and will continue to respond to parental needs, whether conscious or unconscious, expressed or un-expressed. Thus, the disruptive child will continue to be disruptive so long as his/her behavior is reinforced, and the disturbed child will remain disturbed for the same reason, so long as his/her role is essential to the homeostatic balance of the family system. Even such relatively serious offenses as stealing and fire-setting, although outwardly deplored by the family, are often implicitly supported. For example, parents might criticize and make threats of punishment, but fail to follow through; or they might take such unusual interest in the child's misbehavior that she/he is positively rewarded, and the gratification derived from attention in whatever form is reinforcement for repetition of the behavior.

In a way, it is accurate to say that the whole family gives the scapegoat child their approval to act out the unconscious wishes of other members. That this acting out of family tensions (or unconscious wishes) may be carried even to the extreme act of *homicide* has been hypothesized by one researcher (Sargeant, 1968), who conducted an in-depth investigation of nine children who had been referred to juvenile court after having killed a member of their family. Sargeant's research supported the hypothesis that the child who kills is acting as the unwitting lethal agent of an adult (usually a parent) who unconsciously prompts the child to kill so that the parent can vicariously enjoy the benefits of the act (p. 735). Such extreme acting out by the child makes it unnecessary for the parents to confront their own tensions and anxieties.

The scapegoated child bears the projected burden of all that is presently wrong with the family, but more than that, may also be used to "balance out" wrongs and disappointments from years—possibly generations—past. Boszormenyi-Nagy & Ulrich (1981) commented on a patient who had become the scapegoat for her parents' childhood deprivations, and added:

> In such an instance, projection is not the only mechanism at work. The circumstances of relational unfairness and exploitation are factual. The parents see themselves as entitled to draw from the child because they are engaged in some kind of eternal effort at overpayment elsewhere (p. 168).

All families have likes and dislikes, and most parents feel a preference for some of their children over others. In the open-family system, such differences are accepted without particular stress. In a closed family, however, even minor differences can turn into irrational prejudices as they become rigid, fixed, automatized and walled off from the corrective influence of prevailing realities (Ackerman, 1967, p. 52).

Although the prejudicial practice of scapegoating is most often noted in clinical reports of closed families, it has also been described in families like those we are calling *disordered*. The process of scapegoating, however, appears to take different forms in the two types of family. As we have seen, scapegoating in the closed family involves a rigid and relatively fixed role assignment for one particular member, which he or she may bear for life. By contrast, in the disordered family, the scapegoat role, like everything else about the family, is subject to change. According to Ackerman (1967), this scapegoat role does not stand alone, but is part of an interlocking role system that includes *attacker, victim* (scapegoat), and *healer.* These roles are not filled by the same members all the time, but seem to be interchangeable. That is, the victim may become the new attacker, and the former attacker may arise to defend the new victim. In an extremely unstructured family, however, it would seem unlikely that scapegoating could occur, since as Beavers & Voeller (1983) commented, "A considerable degree of cohesion is required to develop mutually acceptable family rules that support scapegoating" (p. 88).

Again, it should be stressed that the scapegoat is not simply an innocent victim of the family, but plays a large part in his or her own selection and continuance in the role. It is, of course, a severely prejudicial role, but one that the scapegoat accepts and supports. This, as we have seen, is what systems theory would predict—that the whole system (family), including the apparent "victim" would act to maintain the system's homeostatic balance, unhealthy though it might be, even at the expense of one element of the system.

Summary of "Relationships in the Family System"

Part III has dealt with relationships in the family system. Chapter 5 described the human needs for both connectedness and autonomy, making the point that although all persons need relationships and suffer without them, each person also needs to feel secure in his or her own sense of being an independent, autonomous entity. In fact, to the person without such a feeling of autonomy, relationships are likely to be unsatisfying, perhaps fearful.

Chapter 6 reviewed several sorts of crippling family relations, touching on themes of dehumanizing relations, sham relations, merged relations, and rigid subject-object role relationships. Chapter 7 explored some pathogenic patterns of family relating often found in severely disturbed families: pseudo-mutuality, mystification, marital schism and marital skew, the over-protective mother and inadequate father combination, perverse triangles, and finally the prejudicial role of family scapegoat.

Among all these disturbed forms of relationships are obvious similarities: each demads the use of deception in some form, a masking of what is really going on, an unawareness of the feelings of others, and an absence of direct, open communication. Significantly, much of the pathology discussed here is a sickness of the system and cannot adequately be explained in terms of the individual dynamics of family members. Families, like all systems, are *adaptive*, striving to keep themselves intact, viable, and in homeostatic balance. Usually the efforts to adapt produce functional and healthy behavior (as when a family "rule" is changed to accommodate changed circumstances), but sometimes adaptation is self-defeating for the system and personally destructive for one or more of its members (as, for example, marital schism); in other cases the family's adaptive behavior serves to benefit the system, but at the expense of an individual member (as in the case of the family scapegoat). In many cases, individual symptoms themselves can be interpreted as the result of attmepts by the system to relieve a difficulty. The point is that adaptation in family systems, like biological systems, is not always healthy or functional. In any event, system's theory would posit that when a pathological relationship or an individual symptom exists in a family, it can best be attributed to the system's efforts to adapt to change, rather than to any "badness or madness" of a member.

What, then, is a healthy family relationship? The answers are certainly not all in, but research to date suggests that the two dimensions of *involvement* and *flexibility* are important determinants. Research by Olson, Sprenkle, & Russell (1979) indicates that on both of these dimensions, the middle ground is preferable (a position of "optimal balance"), while the extremes of both dimensions (overinvolvement and under-involvement; rigidity and structureless chaos) are associated with family system dysfunction. This finding was supported by Russell's (1979) investigation, in which she found that the highest family functioning was associated with moderate family cohesion and flexibility, while low-functioning families had extreme scores on both of these dimensions. Based on such findings, it would appear that the primary criterion for healthy family relationships is moderation—best demonstrated in the family that is open and available for contact with the outside world, but has identifiable and stable boundaries; one whose members are involved and interconnected, but not enmeshed; and one that is flexible, but has structure. The attempt to move families from extreme positions to positions of moderation along the dimensions of flexibility and involvement is a basic concern of family systems therapy, as the next four chapters will show.

REFERENCES

Ackerman, N. W. (1967). Prejudice and scapegoating in the family. In Zuk, G. H., & Boszormenyi-Nagy, I. (Eds.), *Family Therapy and Disturbed Families*, pp. 48–57. Palo Alto: Science & Behavior Books.

Bach, G. R., & Deutsch, R. M. (1970). *Pairing.* New York: Avon.

Bantz, W. R., & Razer, R. A. (1972, December). Why people fall in and out of romantic love. Psychology Today pp. 36–37.

Bateson, G., Jackson, D. D., Haley, J., & Weakland, J. H. (1956). Toward a theory of schizophrenia, *Behavioral Science, 1*, 251–264.

Beavers, W. R., & Voeller, M. N. (1983). Family models: Comparing and contrasting the Olson circumplex model with the Beavers systems model. *Family Process, 22*, 85–98.

Berelson, B., & Steiner, G. A. (1964). Human Behavior. New York: Harcourt.

Boszormenyi-Nagy, I. (1967). Relational modes and meaning. In Zuk, G. H., & Boszormenyi-Nagy, I., (Eds.), *Family Therapy and Disturbed Families*, pp. 53–73. Palo Alto: Science & Behavior books.

Boszormenyi-Nagy, I., & Framo, J. L. (1965). *Intensive Family Therapy.* Hagerstown, Md.: Harper.

Boszormenyi-Nagy, I., & Ulrich, D. N. (1981). Contextual family therapy. In Gurman, A. S., & Kniskern, D. P. (Eds.), *Handbook of Family Therapy*, pp. 151–186. New York: Brunner/Mazel.

Bowen, M. (1961). Family psychotherapy. *The American Journal of Orthopsychiatry, 31*, 40–60.

Carson, R. C. (1969) *Interaction Concepts of Personality.* Chicago: Aldine.

Chapman, A. H. (1968). *Put-Offs and Come-Ons.* New York: Putnam/Berkley.

Dicks, H. V. (1968). Experiences with marital tensions seen in the psychological clinic. In Howells, J. G. (Ed.), *Theory and Practice of Family Psychiatry*, pp. 267–287. Edinburgh: Oliver & Boyd.

Fast, J. (1971). *The Incompatibility of Men and Women.* New York: Avon.

Ferreira, A. J. (1963). Family myth and homeostasis. Archives of General Psychiatry, *9*, 460–464.

Fraser, J. G. (1927). *The Golden Bough.* New York: Macmillan.

Fromm, E. (1956). *The Art of Loving.* New York: Harper.

Fromm-Reichmann, F. (1948). Notes on the development of treatment by psychoanalytic psychotherapy. *Psychiatry, 11,* 267–277.

Fromm-Reichmann, F. (1959). Loneliness. *Psychiatry, 22,* 1–15.

Greenacre, P. (1968). Considerations regarding the parent-infant relationship. In Howells, J. G. (Ed.), *Theory and Practice of Family Psychiatry,* pp. 177–197. Edinburgh: Oliver & Boyd.

Haley, J. (1967). Toward a theory of pathological systems. In Zuk, G. H., & Boszormenyi-Nagy, I. (Eds.), *Family Therapy and Disturbed Families,* pp. 11–27. Palo Alto: Science & Behavior Books.

Hall, C. A., & Lindzey, G. (1947). *Theories of Personality.* New York: John Wiley.

Hebb, D. O. (1960). The American revolution. *American Psychologist, 15,* 735–745.

Henry, J. (1973). *Pathways to Madness.* New York: Random House / Vintage.

Heron, W. (1961). Cognitive and psychological effects of perceptual isolation. In Solomon, P., *Sensory Deprivation: A Symposium at the Harvard Medical School,* pp. 6–33. Cambridge: Harvard University Press.

Horney, K. (1945). *Our Inner Conflicts.* New York: Norton.

Howells, J. G. (1968). *Theory and Practice of Family Psychiatry.* Edinburgh: Oliver & Boyd.

Kernodle, W. R. (1972, December). Romantic love may be on the way out: Comment on Bantz & Raxer. *Psychology Today,* pp. 36–37.

Kiley, D. (1983). *The Peter Pan Syndrome.* New York: Dodd, Mead.

Komarovsky, M. (1967). *Blue-Collar Marriage.* New York: Random House / Vintage.

Laing, R. D. (1965a). *The Divided Self.* Baltimore: Penguin.

Laing, R. D. (1965b). Mystification, confusion and conflict. In Boszormenyi-Nagy, I. & Framo, J. S. (Eds.), *Intensive Family Therapy,* pp. 343–363. Hagerstown, Md.: Harper.

Leary, T. (1957). *Interpersonal Diagnosis of Personality.* New York: Ronald Press.

Lederer, W. J., & Jackson, D. D. (1968). *The Mirages of Marriage.* New York: Norton.

Levy, D. (1943). *Maternal Overprotection.* New York: Columbia University Press.

Lewin, K. (1951). *Field Theory in the Social Sciences.* Cartwright, D. (Ed.). New York: Harper.

Lidz, T., Cornelison, A., Carlson, D., & Fleck, S. (1967). Intrafamilial environment of the schizophrenic patient: The transmission of irrationality. In Handel, G. (Ed.), *The Psychosocial Interior of the Family,* pp. 276–291. Chicago: Aldine.

Lidz, T., Cornelison, A., Fleck, S., & Terry, D. (1957). The intrafamilial environment of the schizophrenic patient: Marital Schism and marital skew. *American Journal of Psychiatry, 114,* 241–248.

Montagu, A. (1961). *Touching: The Human Significance of the Skin.* New York: Harper/Perennial.

Olson, D. H., Sprenkle, D. H., & Russell, C. S. (1979). Circumplex model of marital and family systems: I. Cohesion and adaptability dimensions, family types, and clinical applications. *Family Process, 18,* 3–25.

Putney, A., & Putney, G. J. (1964). *The Adjusted American.* New York: Harper.

Riskin, J. M., & Faunce, E. E. (1972, December). An evaluative review of family interaction research. *Family Process,* pp. 365–455.

Russell, C. S. (1979), Circumplex model of marital and family systems: III. Empirical evaluation with families, *Family Process, 18,* 29–32.

Sargeant, D. (1968). Children who kill—a family conspiracy? In Howells, J. G. (Ed.), *Theory and Practice of Family Psychiatry,* pp. 734–744. Edinburgh: Oliver & Boyd.

Satir, V. (1967). *Conjoint Family Therapy.* Palo Alto: Science & Behavior Books.

Satir, V. (1972). *Peoplemaking.* Palo Alto: Science & Behavior Books.

Spiegel, J. P. (1957). The resolution of role conflict within the family. *Psychiatry, 20,* 1–16.

Spitz, R. (1965). *The First Year of Life.* New York: IU Press.

Sullivan, H. S. (1953). *The Interpersonal Theory of Psychiatry.* New York: Norton.

Tanner, I. J. (1973). *Loneliness: The Fear of Love.* New York: Harper.

Vogel, E. F., & Bell, N. W. (1967). The emotionally disturbed child as the family scapegoat. In Handel, G. (Ed.), *The Psychosocial Interior of the Family,* pp. 424–442. Chicago: Aldine.

Weiss, R. S. (1968). Materials for a theory of social relationships. In Bennis, W. G., Schein, E. W., Steele, F. I., & Berlew, D. E. (Eds.), *Interpersonal Dynamics,* pp. 154–163. Homewood, Ill.: Dorsey Press.

White, R. N. (1964). *The Abnormal Personality.* New York: Ronald Press.

Wynne, L., Ryckoff, L., Day, J., & Hirsch, S. (1958). Pseudo-mutuality in the family relations of schizophrenics. *Psychiatry, 71,* 205–220.

PART IV

TREATMENT OF TROUBLED FAMILIES: SYSTEMS MODELS OF THERAPY

The Interactional View

BACKGROUND

Early in the decade 1952–1962 an unusual group of people assembled at Menlo Park, California, under the direction of anthropologist Gregory Bateson. The group was originally funded to study the paradoxes of abstraction in communication, but later extended its focus to include schizophrenic communication specifically, and then interaction process and patterns in families with schizophrenic members. In addition to Bateson, the team included Jay Haley, a communication specialist; John Weakland, an engineer-turned-anthropologist; and psychiatrists William Fry and Don Jackson.

In 1959 a separate but related research group was formed in Palo Alto under the direction of Don Jackson to study schizophrenia and the family. Called the Mental Research Institute (MRI), this second project originally included psychiatrist Jules Riskin and Virginia Satir, a psychiatric social worker. These were later joined by Haley and Weakland from the Bateson project and by Paul Watzlawick, an Austrian psychologist and a student of language and symbolic logic. Although Bateson was never officially associated with the MRI, his influence was strongly felt in both projects. In addition, both groups shared an interest in human communication and the part it played in the etiology of schizophrenia.

Members of these two projects brought together vastly different philosophies and backgrounds, but ultimately created a unified conceptual framework that has come to be known as "the interactional view," with Weakland and Watzlawick as its primary spokesmen. Contributing influences were those as diverse as Harry Stack Sullivan's interpersonal theory, von Bertalanffy's general system theory, Norbert Weiner's cybernetic model, Viktor Frankl's "paradoxical intention," and Russell and Whitehead's mathematical Theory of Logical Types—all adding a richness to the final expression of the interactional view.

Although the Bateson group was not primarily concerned with treatment, its research and theory-building produced a new way of conceptualizing human problems. Departing from the monadic, intrapsychic view held by most therapists at that time, the group adopted a theoretical stance that was essentially a systems view, involving information, cybernetics, and the processing of communication within systems (Watzlawick & Weakland, 1977, p. xii).

Weakland informally recalled how this conceptual view influenced the kind of therapy done at the Mental Research Institute:

> Lo and behold, it looked to us as if we didn't have to go back to the time when patients were little kids. It seemed that in a number of respects, we could discern and describe how the crazy ways the patients are talking *now* hang together with—in a way make sense or fit with—the way other family members are talking right now. (Weakland, 1981, p. 54)

Early theoretical developments tended to follow this systemic view, particularly the work of Jackson regarding family homeostasis, negative and positive feedback, rules and metarules, and circular causality.

In 1956 the Bateson team published a landmark article (Bateson, Jackson, Haley, & Weakland, 1956) that introduced the concept of the "double bind" as an explanation for the occurrence of schizophrenia. (This family communicative pattern will be discussed further in Chapter 13.)

In 1967 members of the MRI published a fully developed expression of theory growing out of their experiences with families. The book, *Pragmatics of Human Communication*, represents a synthesis of communication theory, system theory, and psychopathology, with a smattering of philosophy, literature, and mathematics. Among other important contributions, this book introduced the five Axioms of Communication, three of which have already been reviewed in Chapter 4. Briefly, the five axioms are:

Axiom #1: One cannot *not* communicate.

Axiom #2: Every communication has a content and a relational aspect, so that the latter classified the former and is therefore a metacommunication.

Axiom #3: The nature of a relationship is contingent upon the punctuation of the communicational sequences between the communicants.

Axiom #4: Human beings communicate both *digitally* and *analogically*. This is quite similar to the distinction discussed in Chapter 4 between sign and symbol usage. Digital communication, like symbol communication, is based on arbitrarily assigned codes that need bear no resemblance to the thing symbolized. (As Watzlawick, Beavin, and Jackson (1967) point out, there is nothing particularly cat-like in the letters c-a-t, just as there is nothing five-like in the numeral 5.) Digital communication is essential for describing or talking about objects, but is inadequate for dealing with relationships. Analogic communication, like sign communication, is believed to be more archaic, and is tied directly to the thing it stands for. For the most part, words are digital (symbolic), and nonverbal communication (sign) is analogic. As noted in Chapter 4, human beings, alone, of all animals, have the capacity to use both analogic *and digital communication.*

Axiom #5: All communicational interchanges are either *symmetrical* or *complementary* in the relationship they imply, depending on whether they suggest equality or difference. Relationships in which partners strive for sameness are called symmetrical; relationships which depend on difference for their existence (mother-child, dominant-submissive, teacher-student) are called complementary.

When the Bateson project ended in the 1960s, Bateson gave up psychiatry and went off to study dolphins in the Virgin Islands; Jackson died in 1968; Weakland and Haley, who as early as 1955 had begun to study the therapeutic techniques of the extraordinary hypnotherapist Milton Erickson, continued their work in this direction, ultimately incorporating Erickson's approach into the interactional view.

PREMISES OF THE INTERACTIONAL VIEW

Although much has been written, independently and collectively, by the prolific scholars associated with the interactional view, it was not until 1981 that Carol Wilder-Mott, a long-time student of Bateson's work, undertook to formalize the premises that underlie its theory and the practice of therapy associated with it (Wilder-Mott & Weakland, 1981, pp. 23–30). These are:

(1) *Premise of Systemic Description.* A system model of behavior and change focuses upon what is currently happening within the interactional system of one's interpersonal network, with little regard for forces "inside" the individual or for uncovering past traumas. Emphasis is on observable behavior in the present, rather than on history. The systemic view holds that causality is circular rather than linear, so a

system's behavior can be independent of its history—its behavior is determined solely by its state at any given time.

(2) *Premise of Pragmatism.* Action is primary; theory is secondary. MRI therapists took the position that it was their primary job to *do* therapy, and only secondarily to *explain* the doing. Commenting on this viewpoint, Wilder-Mott (1981) adds: "We can speak a proper sentence without being able to parse it; tie a knot with no knowledge of the neurophysiology involved; bake a cake understanding neither chemistry nor thermodynamics" (p. 26). This premise probably accounted for the great number of practical strategies for solving human problems that grew out of the work of the MRI and particularly its Brief Therapy Center.

The premise of pragmatism also included as a corollary what has been termed the *premise of possibility*, which takes issue with the popularly-accepted "utopia syndrome," described by Watzlawick as a "problem-engendering pattern resulting when the ideal is mistaken for the possible" (Watzlawick, Weakland, & Fisch, 1974, pp. 47–61). The premise of possibility is explained further by Wilder-Mott:

> This position is based upon the belief that life, at best, is fraught with difficulties and challenges ... The myths of Horatio Alger, Hollywood, and the human potential movement still prevail in middle-class American culture, promoting the belief that anything less than a life which moves from peak experience to peak experience is somehow lacking. While it might be unreasonable to suggest working for less than the best life, more brutal to the human spirit is the relentless pursuit of chimerical bliss ... The premise of possibility does not compel one to abandon hopes, dreams, ideals, or visions of the best human condition; rather it directs one simply to consider the difference between what is possible to achieve within a given set of constraints and what is not, and to act accordingly. (p. 27)

(3) *Premise of Verbal Realism.* There is no single reality. "Reality" depends on the point of veiw, and our reality is constructed through communication. Therapeutic strategies

do not intend to alter facts, but to alter the *meaning* attributed to the facts.

THERAPY AND CHANGE

From its beginning, the Mental Research Institute had been involved in doing, studying, and teaching family therapy, but in 1967 the MRI Brief Therapy Center was founded for the specific purpose of studying family therapy still further—to increase the effectiveness and efficiency of methods currently being used.

Because of the diverse backgrounds of MRI members, there is no single therapeutic approach that can be attributed to them as a group. As Wilder-Mott commented: "the interactional approach includes almost as much divergence as convergence" (Wilder-Mott & Weakland, 1981, p. 23). Satir conceptualized and treated a family's problems in terms of communication and self-esteem; Haley saw family interaction as a power struggle and the occurrence of symptoms as ways of controlling the relationship; Jackson stressed the family's system properties of feedback, homeostasis, rules, and metarules; Weakland examined a family's problem-solving methods. Somehow it all fitted together.

Goals of Therapy

In its early days, MRI's Brief Therapy Center did not specify any general treatment goals except to resolve the presenting problem, as seen and described by the patient(s). This means that the therapist accepted whatever the patient offered, and looked for *what* was happening to maintain the problem, avoiding asking *why*. The second goal developed later and involved the MRI's concept of change as being of two orders (these have already been mentioned in Chapter 1): *First-order change* occurs when there is a shifting withing the system—a change that ultimately makes no difference to the system. For example, a schizophrenic son may undergo therapy and get better, but soon another child in the family begins to develop symptoms. Even though first-order change occurs in the form of the improvement of a member, the family *system* is not inproved. *Second-order change* is a shift that actually alters the system. This last is the goal of interactional therapy and one that requires the intervention of someone outside the system, usually a therapist. As mentioned in Chapter 1, a system in trouble is trapped in its own "game without end," a situation that Watzlawick & Weakland (1977) described as one in which the system cannot generate from within itself the rules for the change of its rules. Consequently, they say, "such a system will endlessly run through the finite number of internal changes available to it, thereby achieving only more of the same without ever arriving at a resolution of the impasse. The metarule for systemic change can, therefore, be introduced only from the outside, and this is what interventions in interactional psychotherapy are all about." (p. 249)

Principles of Interactional Therapy

In describing how therapy was conducted at the Institute's Brief Therapy Center, four of its members (Weakland, Fisch, Watzlawick, & Bodin, 1974) compiled a list of main principles which are summarized here. These are consistent with system theory, pragmatics, and verbal realism.

(1) We are frankly system-oriented, in a broad sense. The presenting problem offers, in one package, what the patient is ready to work on, a concentrated manifestation of whatever is wrong and a concrete index of any progress made.

(2) We view the problems that people bring to psychotherapists as situational difficulties between people—problems of interaction.

(3) We regard such problems as primarily an outcome of everyday difficulties—usually involving adaptation to some life change—that have been mishandled by the parties involved.

(4) While fortuitous life difficulties—such as illness, ac-

cident, or loss of job—somehow appear to initiate the development of a problem, we see normal transitional steps in family living as the most common and important "everyday difficulties" that may lead to problems. These transitions include: the change from the voluntary relationship of courtship to the commitment of marriage, and from the commitment of marriage to the less reversible commitment when the first child is born; the sharing of influence with other authorities that is required when a child enters school, and with both child and peers in the adolescent period; the shift from a child-oriented marital relationship back to a two-party system when the child leaves home, and the intensification of the effect of this shift at retirement; and, finally, the return to single life at the death of a spouse.

(5) We see two main ways by which "problems" are likely to develop—treating an ordinary difficulty as a "problem," or treating an ordinary (or worse) difficulty as no problem at all—that is, by either overemphasizing or underemphasizing the difficulties of living.

(6) We assume that one a difficulty begins to be seen as a "problem," the continuation, and often the exacerbation of this problem results from the creation of positive feedback loop, most often centered around those very behaviors of the individual in the system that are intended to resolve the difficulty: The original difficulty is met with an attempted "solution" that intensifies the original difficulty, and so on. This can be illustrated with the example of the typical rebellious teenager, who, when faced with parental discipline, will increase his/her rebelliousness, which in turn is likely to increase repressive action by parents, which then makes the teenager even more rebellious, and so on (Fisch, Watzlawick, Weakland, & Bodin, 1977, p. 318).

(7) We view long-standing problems or symptoms not as "chronicity," but as persistence of a *repetitively* poorly handled difficulty.

(8) We see the resolution of problems as primarily requiring a substitution of behavior patterns so as to interrupt the vicious, positive feedback circles.

(9) We seek means of promoting beneficial changes that work, even if our remedies appear illogical. For instance, we would be likely to comment on how sad a depressed patient

looks and to suggest that there must be some real and important reason for this. Once given some information on the situation, we might say it is rather strange that s/he is not even *more* depressed. The usual result, paradoxical as it may seem, is that the patient begins to look and sound better.

(10) In addition to accepting what the patient offers, we "think small" by focusing on the symptom and working in a limited way toward its relief.

(11) Our approach is fundamentally pragmatic. We try to base our conceptions and interventions on direct observation in the treatment situation of *what* is going on in systems of human interaction, *how* the systems continue to function in such ways, and *how* they can be altered most effectively. The question of *why* is not relevant and is avoided (Weakland, Fisch, Watzlawick, & Bodin, 1974).

Therapeutic Interventions

Consistent with the stated premises and principles, and with the expressed goals of interactional therapy widely ranging techniques were developed or adopted by the MRI group. In general the therapist usually controls the session, tending to be active and directive.

Three of the most useful and innovative of their interventions are (1) relabeling (reframing), (2) directing behavior change through "homework assignments," and (3) using paradoxical instructions in the form of symptom prescriptions. Briefly described below, these interventions are more involved than this limited description suggests, and their application requires considerable skill.

Relabeling (Reframing)

It has long been accepted by students of perceptual psychology that we never deal with realities *per se* but with images—that is, with our perceptions and interpretations of those perceptions. The solutions we select tend to be "more of the same," unless we can break the illusionary frame and step outside the box of our perceptions and experience a new reality. Reframing thus means to change the conceptual viewpoint in relation to which a situation is experienced, and put it in another frame which fits the facts equally well, but changes the meaning. For instance, Tom Sawyer's fence-painting is reframed from a tiresome task to fun. (As you remember, in Mark Twain's classic, Tom manipulated his friend, Huckleberry Finn, into taking over the fence-painting by pretending it was enjoyable—a task he would give up only reluctantly.) Thus, in its simplest terms, therapeutic relabeling means presenting patient behavior in positive terms in order to avoid the appearance of criticism or blame. Barton & Alexander (1981) provide other examples of reframing:

> For example, rigid or authoritarian fathers can be portrayed as active leaders; people who do not disclose their feelings can be relabeled as not withholding, but rather considerate of laying their problems on others; "disrespectful" teenagers can be portrayed as struggling with their autonomy....The goal of ... relabeling is ... not to represent the "truth" to family members but rather to portray family members and their behavior in ways that will better fit family members' desired expectations. Family members are more willing to accept a view of the world which leaves them blameless and which suggests they are not cruel or malevolent to each other. In turn, family members are more likely to change their cognitive labels, affective reactions and behavior toward one another if the therapist "paints a picture" which portrays family members in ways they would like to perceive each other....A mother who experiences guilt or perceives herself as a failure is presumably relieved to hear that her son's acting-out represents his "struggle for independence," rather than a "rejection" of her. Similarly, father and other family members presumably experience a different affective reaction that father "assumes major responsibility" in a family, than to hearing "he's so bossy, he won't let anybody else make a decision." (pp. 422–423)

Homework Assignments (Directed Behavior Change)

Because the aim of interactional therapy is to change behavior, authoritative directions are sometimes given to patients in an effort to get them to stop doing things that maintain the problem or to do other things that may relieve the problem. These instructions are about matters that may appear minor to the patient, although to the therapist they appear "a microcosm of the central difficulty." (Watzlawick &

Weakland, 1977, p. 289). An example would be when a patient who avoids making any demands of others in his personal relationships is assigned the task of asking for *one* gallon of gas at a service station, specifically requesting each of the usual free services, and offering a twenty-dollar bill in payment. Such instructions are to be carried out between sessions, in real-life situations, and reported at the next session (Watzlawick & Weakland, 1977).

Symptom Prescriptions

This technique is based on the concept of paradox and is a form of therapeutic double bind, in which the patient is instructed to do *more* of whatever is perceived as a troublesome symptom. For example, a disruptive child is told that he is to be as disruptive and uncooperative as possible. He soon tires of following the instructions and stops his disruptive activities. This technique is drawn from hypnotherapist Milton Erickson, who used it, for example, with a nail-biting child by directing him to *increase* his nail-biting until what had been, for the child, a delightful way of irritating his parents, now became more of a chore, which he resisted and eventually abandoned.

Before concluding this summary of the techniques of psychotherapy growing out of the interactional view, special mention should be made of the work of Virginia Satir, one of the most influential and charismatic of family therapists, and one who in large measure is responsible for popularization of the family therapy movement. Although one of the original members of the MRI and greatly influenced by the systems approach of the Palo Alto group, she retained her own view of family interaction, which perhaps can best be identified as a communication emphasis, with focus on the individual, but always within the context of the family. In treating families, she stresses improvement of their communication skills: being congruent and open, asking for what you want, and being clear, direct, and specific in interaction with one another. The goals of improved communication are always to build a sense of self-worth in the individual, reduce family pain and suffering, and bring about positive changes in the way members interact.

SUMMARY

Although the interactional view evolved largely out of the epistemology of Gregory Bateson, it eventually incorporated the work of many different people and viewpoints, becoming a synthesis of communication theory, general system theory, and applied psychotherapy. It is systemic, pragmatic, and focused on communication. Many of its original contributors have moved on to other things, but the overall work of the Bateson group and MRI group, a unique blend of research, training, and clinical accomplishments—remains an impressive contribution to the field of family communication and one that has greatly influenced other students of the family system.

CHAPTER 9

Haley's Strategic Model of Family Therapy

BACKGROUND

There are many "strategic approaches" to family therapy, most of which would be relevant to a discussion of system-based treatment because they all start with the premise that individual symptoms are manifestations of dysfunctional relationships in the family. This chapter will limit its review to the work of communications specialist Jay Haley, an early member of the Bateson research project and a pioneer in family therapy. The influence of his association with Bateson and later with the Mental Research Institute is apparent in his work.

Although strategic therapy has not fully developed theory of its own, as does Bowen's therapy for instance, it draws from cybernetic theory, information theory, and communication theory, and has deep roots in the family therapy movement of the early 1950s.

More than other systems therapists, Haley opposed *intrapsychic* explanations of pathology, emphasizing instead the dysfunctional relationships and communicative patterns within the system where pathology occurs. Emphasis is more on technique than on theory—particularly on techniques that have proved to be effective and workable. Like the interactional approach just discussed, Haley's approach is completely pragmatic. As Haley commented, "Research investigators require complex theories; clinicians need simple ones" (Haley, 1976, p. 100).

In developing his strategic approach, Haley was strongly influenced by three sources. The first, of course, was Bateson, an intellectual force in the MRI, and by co-workers in the Bateson project, notably Weakland and Jackson. A second important influence in the development of strategic therapy, especially with regard to techniques of paradoxical intervention, was Milton Erickson, the internationally acclaimed psychiatrist and medical hypnotherapist, with whom Haley had become acquainted in the 1960s and whom he visited frequently in Phoenix. Haley was especially impressed by the dicovery that Erickson, quite independently of the Bateson group, was using double binds as therapeutic measures in his practice. The third influence was Salvador Minuchin—with whom Haley worked later at the Philadelphia Child Guidance Clinic—whose "structural" approach to family therapy is acknowledged by Haley as having been influential in his own work.

SOME PRINCIPLES OF STRATEGIC THERAPY

(1) By definition, strategic therapy is that in which the therapist initiates activities, designs the approach to be used, and takes responsibility for the outcome. The therapist is active and directive, never passive or "client-centered." In

Haley's words, "He [the therapist] must identify solvable problems, set goals, design interventions to achieve the goals, examine the responses he receives to correct his approach, and ultimately examine the outcome of his therapy to see if it has been effective" (Haley, 1973, p. 17).

(2) Therapy is brief and intensive, rarely long-term.

(3) Insight or awareness on the part of the patient is not important in strategic therapy, and there is little concern for unconscious processes.

(4) Strategic therapy takes into account the family developmental process and the points of crisis that arise at each stage. Symptoms appear whenever there is an interruption in the flow from stage to stage. The family sometimes becomes "stuck" and unable to make a successful transition to the next stage. The usual points at which such interruptions occur are: courtship, marriage, childbirth, child-rearing, middle-marriage, weaning parents from children, and retirement/old age.

(5) Therapeutic focus is usually on the family member who has been identified by the other members as a problem. Although the therapist may be aware that this person is only the symptom-bearer who expresses the system's dysfunction, the therapist accepts the patient's stated problem and works with it. Change in only one member may be sufficient to start a chain reaction of change in the entire system.

(6) Focus is on the identified patient, but the strategic therapist is also concerned with dysfunctional relationships as reflected in communication patterns and sequences. Haley cites an example of a marital pattern of relating that has rigidified:

> A couple that is limited in range can follow only one pattern. For example, the wife may be able to take care of the husband, but they cannot shift, allowing the husband to take care of her. Therefore, if the wife becomes ill, the husband must become more ill so that she can continue to take care of him since that is the only behavior pattern they have. (Haley, 1976, p. 159)

Patterns also build around power issues—expressing who is in control and how he/she holds on to the power. Communication defines who controls the relationship, and symptoms are sometimes used as strategies for control in the marital dyad or the family. Of particular import is Haley's recognition that messages are attempts to define the relationship, and the primary issue in all human relationships is who sets the rules, or, more precisely, who is to *decide* who sets the rules. With this recognition, it is easy to see that the passive member may actually be in control of the relationship and, as Ronald Fox (1976) wrote:

> " ... by defining the relationship as one in which he is to be passive, the "victim" at a metacommunicative level is also saying, 'I am in charge of saying who is in charge here and I decide that you must be in charge.' In this way the 'passive victim' may wield much control while appearing to be helpless." (p. 476)

(7) This is an *analogic* approach, in which a symptom is seen as a communicative act that is metaphorical in nature. An analogy is a statement that means something about something else; thus a man's chronic headache may represent a relational problem with a wife who is a "headache" to him, or conflict between two members may be a metaphor for unexpressed conflict between other members (Madanes, 1984). Only by understanding the metaphor and the metaphorical sequences in a family's interaction can strategies be developed to solve their problem.

GOALS OF STRATEGIC THERAPY

The general goal of strategic therapy is to make the system unstable by (1) changing the behavior of the identified patient, and (2) changing the interaction patterns and sequences among family members, thereby creating disequilibrium in the system. The family is always aware of the first goal and collaborates in formulating it, but the second may be the therapist's private goal which he/she does not share with the family. When the system becomes unstable, customary ways of interacting and controlling no longer work and the members must find new patterns, thus achieving therapeutic change.

STRATEGIES OF THERAPY

The strategies of this model closely resemble those of the interactional model; the difference seems to be one of degree. The therapist who follows a strategic model is more authoritarian in making assignments, more "manipulative" in assigning paradoxical tasks, and more extreme in reframing. Openness, straightforward communication, and guilelessness are not requirements of the strategic therapist. Proponents of the interactional view have commented about strategic therapists:

> ... certain colleagues of ours seem almost proud to play chameleons; they employ something akin to judo techniques, using the nature and direction of human system's pathology to bring about its own downfall. Thus, instead of disarming their patients with the counterthrust of their sincerity, they are likely to yield and in yielding, to manipulate. (Fisch, et al., 1977, p. 315)

The following subsections describe three of the specific therapeutic strategies used, again with the caution that these are considerably more complex than it is possible to explain here, and should be attempted only with appropriate training.

Assigning Tasks the Therapist Wants the Family to Carry Out

There are times when a direct and forceful assignment is made—one that the family is expected to carry out fully and without fail (Haley, 1976, p. 52). An example of when this might be useful is the case of overinvolvement in a parent-child dyad, with a peripheral parent who is scarcely involved at all. Interference with this relational pattern would create extreme anxiety in the members and disequilibrium in the system. So the strategic therapist deliberately sets about doing just that by giving task instructions, which the family is required to follow. Haley (1976) provides examples of such assignments:

• In the case of a controlling mother who is overinvolved with her son, the *father* and son are asked to do some minor thing that the mother would not approve of. (Note that it will be difficult for the mother to arrange what they do when the thing must be something that she does not want.)

• A father who is always siding with his small daughter against his wife may be required to wash the sheets when the daughter wets the bed. (This will tend to disengage daughter and father *or* cure the bedwetting.) (p. 60)

To insure that the tasks are carried out as assigned, a report is always required at the next visit; patients are never permitted to avoid assignments without severe comment from the therapist.

Assigning Tasks the Therapist Does Not Want the Family to Carry Out

This, as we have already seen, is the "paradoxical inter-vention" and relates to the more complete discussion of paradox in Chapter 13, particularly the nature of the para-doxical injunction—one that gives an order that cannot be obeyed without disobeying it ("ignore this sign"). This was described by the Bateson group (Bateson, Jackson, Haley, & Weakland, 1956) as a pathological form of communication that frequently is noted in families with a schizophrenic member, and was the underlying factor in the double-bind theory of schizophrenia developed by Bateson's team. In strategic therapy, Haley has turned the paradoxical injunction to significant *therapeutic* use. The therapist may give in-structions that s/he feels certain the family will resist, and in so resisting, the family changes for the better. A paradoxical intervention usually requires that the family members continue to do whatever they are now doing, with the requirement that they *not* change, as: "Keep on fighting." Based on the family's assumed resistance to following instructions and an inherent need in many families to "prove the therapist wrong," they may elect to *stop* fighting, which is a therapeutic gain. If, on the other hand, they *do* follow instructions and keep on fighting, they will have obeyed orders and will have lost control, which destabilizes the system and makes it vulnerable to change. In other words, the therapist gives instructions s/he expects the patients to resist; whether they follow instructions or resist, they will experience change. This is the therapeutic paradox. (It means also, incidentally, that the therapist cannot take credit for family improvement that occurs as a result; rather, the family must be able to say, "See what we have done for ourselves.")

This use of paradoxical intervention is derived directly from hypnosis, wherein the hypnotist encourages the resistance of a subject as a way of inducing trance or deepening the trance. As Haley commented in discussing Erickson's therapeutic use of paradox, "If the subject is asked to have his hand get *lighter* and he says, 'My hand is getting *heavier*,' the hypnotist does not say, 'Now cut that out!' Instead he accepts that response and even encourages it by saying, 'That's fine, you can get heavier yet'" (Haley, 1973, p. 24). Thus, whatever the subject does, it is interpreted as cooperating—a classic bind in a positive rather than a negative form.

Reframing

A variation of paradoxical intervention is to make only positive interpretations of whatever the patient says. As we have already seen, reframing means relabeling patient behavior in positive terms in order to avoid the appearance of criticism and to relieve the patient or the family of blame and quilt. In reframing, whatever the family does is interpreted as having been done for the right reasons ("noble ascriptions"). Whatever symptom occurs has some positive aspects and these are noted and commented on by the therapist. In a similar way, a patient's reported defects and problems are redefined as assets and his "setbacks" in therapy are redefined as progress. In this way the patient's defenses are reduced, he feels understood, and being under no pressure to change, he—paradoxically—can change more readily.

SUMMARY

Haley's views are strongly systems-based, opposing intrapsychic explanations of pathology in favor of relational, interactional, and communicative concerns. Individual symptoms are regarded as responses to the context in which they occur. Therapy focuses on the individual patient and his/her described complaint, but treatment always takes into account the patient's family relationships, especially power and control issues. The therapist is directive in the assignment of tasks for family members. These are intended to destabilize the system, create disequilibrium, and thus facilitate change.

Haley's work has been important in formulating the category of "disqualifying response" in Chapter 13, and in the description of the "disordered" family in Chapter 14.

CHAPTER 10

Bowen's Family Systems Theory and Therapy

No discussion of family systems would be complete without mention of Murray Bowen, who has contributed so much to both the theory and practice of family therapy. Although his definition of a "system" differs somewhat from that of Bertalanffy's General System Theory, his approach is still systemic, patterned after natural systems and consistent with biology and natural sciences. He was one of the earliest theorists to focus on the family as a source of disturbance in the individual member and to conceptualize how relational patterns are associated with the etiology of schizophrenia.

BACKGROUND

Bowen started his career with a psychoanalytic orientation (as it apparent from his use of such terms as "undifferentiated family ego mass"), but soon began seriously to question traditional psychoanalytic thinking. Working with schizophrenic patients at the Menninger Clinic in the 1950s, he began to concentrate on the mother-patient symbiosis (which he called "emotional stuck-togetherness") that so frequently was a part of the history of schizophrenic patients. He soon came to believe that the symbiosis was only part of a larger emotional system in which the whole family was involved. His Family Systems Theory starts with the assumption that schizophrenia is simply a symptom of the whole family's disturbance. After a move to the National Institute of Mental Health in 1954, Bowen introduced there a program in which whole families were hospitalized, creating a worldwide interest in the family therapy movement. The practice of treating whole families caught on rapidly, although practitioners of this new form often had a limited basis for understanding conceptually what they were doing. Bowen's Family Systems Theory provided a needed theoretical base for family group treatment.

FAMILY SYSTEMS THEORY: EIGHT INTERLOCKING CONCEPTS

Family systems theory contains two interrelated variables upon which the whole theory rests: (1) the individual's level of differentiation, and (2) the amount of anxiety in the individual's emotional field. The significance of these variables will become clearer when we review the eight interlocking concepts that make up the theory.

Bowen's theory also postulates that there are two natural forces operating in human relationships: individuality (autonomy) and togetherness (fusion). (This, of course, is an idea that we have encountered in earlier chapters—one that is recognized in concept by most family theorists.)

The family, according to Bowen's view, is always dynamic; like any system, its components are constantly interacting to achieve a satisfactory balance of closeness and separation. Too much of one will trigger attempts to regain the other. This, you will recognize as a homeostatic function, as we have seen in earlier chapters. When applied to a family system, this means that as members have individual needs for both autonomy and closeness, so the family system has counterbalancing forces toward fusion *and* toward the independence of its members. Imbalance in either direction creates a homeostatic urge in the opposite direction in order for the system to regain balance. The balance achieved is not always optimal, however, and the system may rigidify in either of two extreme directions: a state of fusion or merger, in which any move of an individual member toward independence is punished, or a state where members display extreme individuality or separation, where any show of closeness or intimacy is punished. Both of these dysfunctional emotional states are maintained by interaction within the system.

Bowen's theory is composed of eight interlocking concepts, which together explain family systems pathology (Kerr, 1981, pp. 241–252). The first six were part of Bowen's original theory; the last two were added later.

Concept #1: Triangles. Whenever a dyadic relationship becomes unstable, and anxiety and tension occur, at a certain level of emotional intensity the two persons involved will attempt to draw in a third person to form a triad, or triangle (or the third person may be programmed to initiate the involvement when he or she senses tension). Children are most often used in this third-party role when conflict occurs in a marital dyad. It is important to note that the greater the fusion of the family, the greater the potential for anxiety, and the more likely the couple is to engage in such "triangling." If the couple comes to therapy, the therapist himself may be triangled—drawn into taking sides with one or the other partner. The family system may include many triangles, often overlapping, that will appear whenever stress occurs between any two members.

Concept #2: Nuclear Family Emotional Process. This means that whenever tension builds in a family system, there are four potential ways of responding in order to reduce the tension. The more fusion in the family, the greater the need for these devices. They are regarded as dysfunctional because, although they may serve to restore equilibrium, they usually do so at the expense of one or more of the members. The four ways to reduce tension are:

(1) Get away from the other (emotional distancing). A kind of reactivity that can include physical distancing—not even looking at one other—or communicative distancing, that is, treating the other as though he/she does not exist. This seems to be a way of reducing anxiety about being too close and is characteristic of parents of schizophrenic children, where for a time the couple alternates periods of over-closeness with periods of extreme distance, but ultimately settles on distancing. This is what Bowen called "emotional divorce," when it occurs in the marital context.

(2) Marital conflict. This is another way of resolving the needs for both closeness and individuality. It is typical of intense relationships in which the pattern shows fluctuating periods of over-closeness, fighting, and distancing again. The obvious hurtfulness of the fights seems to be balanced by the benefit of anxiety-reduction, after which both parties experience relief for a time, only to build up to a fight again.

(3) Spouse dysfunction. Another technique to reduce tension in the system is for one spouse habitually to give in or compromise himself/herself in order to preserve harmony. While this may accomplish its goal for the benefit of the system, it may also result in impairment in the compromised partner's sense of self, with resulting physical or mental dysfunction. Spouse dysfunction may take the form of either overfunctioning or underfunctioning, and grows out of the unrealistic assumption of one partner that he or she is solely responsible for keeping peace in the family.

(4) Impairment of children. When tension and anxiety occur between spouses, conflict between them can sometimes be avoided if they focus their attention on a child or children, rather than on the true nature of the tension. This is especially likely to occur with couples who are undifferen-

tiated (merged). The focused-on child may then become reactive and vulnerable to pathology of his or her own. (The use of other tension-reducing devices, such as conflict or spouse dysfunction, may serve to spare the child or children.) This, of course, can be recognized as what others have called the "scapegoating" of a child, and has been discussed in Chapter 7.

Concept #3: Family Projection Process. This is the means by which undifferentiation is passed on from parent to child. To illustrate, a mother may project her fears about herself (perhaps "stupid and inadequate") onto a child, and will then treat him as if he in fact had those attributes, at the same time engaging in "anxious hovering" over the focused-on child. The child, in turn, reacts to her interpretation of him and becomes anxious (feeling himself perhaps to be stupid and inadequate), and may begin to engage in behavior that confirms the mother's view of him. The child in this case should not be perceived as simply a victim, for, as we have seen before, once the process has started, he/she participates in its perpetuation.

In the next chapter, you will notice that this family projection process is much like that described by Laing as "pseudo-confirmation" (Laing, 1961, p. 83), when a child is confirmed, not for what he really is, but in the image that the other holds of him. The child, of course, may "know" that he is not as his parent sees him, but fears to displease her by insisting on his own identity.

Concept #4: Differentiation of Self. Even before the advent of family therapy, it had long been noted that a symbiotic attachment frequently exists between schizophrenic patients and their mothers, a closeness Bowen described as "emotional Siamese twins," and this attachment had been believed important in the etiology of schizophrenia. Bowen's studies of hospitalized whole-families suggested that this mother-patient symbiosis was only a fragment of a larger family over-involvement. Bowen (1965) describes his observations:

> Family relationships alternated between overcloseness and overdistance. In the emotional closeness phases the intra-psychic systems of involved family members were so

intimately fused that differentiation of one from the other was impossible. The fusion involved the entire range of ego functioning. One ego could function for that of another. One family member could accurately know the thoughts, fantasies, feelings, and dreams of the other. One family member could become physically ill in response to an emotional stress in another . . . Another manifestation of the family oneness was the spontaneous, fluid shifting of ego strengths and weaknesses from one member to a-nother. Part of a "pathology" could be in one family member and other parts in other family members. It suggested a family jigsaw puzzle of strengths and weak-nesses, with each family member holding pieces of the same puzzle and with considerable trading of pieces . . . Research observation suggested that the larger family emotional oneness had the same basic characteristics as the mother-patient symbiosis. Terms such as "emotional fusion," "emotional connectedness," "emotional stuck-to-getherness," and "ego fusion" all accurately describe the phenomenon. The "symbiotic" hypothesis was discarded and thinking was directed to a larger family phenomenon." (p. 217)

According to this concept, children grow up to achieve different levels of differentiation of self from the family fusion. Some can separate themselves sufficiently to achieve maturity with separate-ego functioning; others remain trapped in the "undifferentiated ego mass," and are more likely to become schizophrenic.

Bowen's measurement of individual differentiation of self is in the form of a subjective scale that indicates the member's point on a continuum, ranging from highest to lowest levels of personal differentiation, i.e., the extent to which the member has achieved an "optimum mix" of togetherness and in-dividuation.

Concept #5: Multigenerational Transmission Process. Early in his career, Bowen expressed the view that schizo-phrenia is a process that spans three generations before being manifest in the psychotic behavior of an individual. This view is a denial of the earlier-held opinion of other theorists that the "schizophrenogenic mother" was the direct linear *cause* of psychosis in a child. "Schizophrenia," in Bowen's formula-tion, "is a by-product of a long series of compromises the system has made, compromises that stabilized the whole at the expense of some of its parts" (Kerr, 1981, p. 248). More explicitly, a parent's level of differentiation can be transmitted to a child. For instance, a woman who is unable to differentiate adequately between intellectual and emotional functioning will tend to marry a man with a similar low level of differentiation. Among their children, one will be of lower differentiation than the others, and this child will also tend to marry a person who is a low differentiator; both then project their low level onto their child, who shows such intense fusion of his emotional and intellectual systems that it is impossible for him to function normally. Consequently, schizophrenia or other disorders (physical, social, emotional) may develop.

Concept #6: Emotional Cutoff. This is the way some people try to deal with their fused family of origin. It is an extreme "solution" in which they try to reduce anxiety created by too much togetherness by going to the opposite extreme and separating themselves totally from the original family system, or at least avoiding all emotionally laden areas in family interaction. In reality, however, this tactic solves nothing because the individual who uses cutoff from parents will still carry with him or her into future relationships the same intense fear of loss of self. This individual will eventually involve himself/herself in other equally threatening relationships, breaking them off abruptly when they become too intense, never satisfying his or her strong relational needs.

Concept #7: Sibling Position. A child's personality is molded by the position he/she holds in relation to other siblings in the family—oldest, youngest, middle child, or whatever. The traits acquired because of position are carried into later relationships, so that, for example, the marriage of an oldest child to a youngest child has predictable consequences in terms of responsibility, decision-making, conflict, and control. The greater the emotional fusion in the relationship, the more the exaggeration of positional traits that can be expected to errupt.

Concept #8: Societal Emotional Process. This is simply an extension to the broader societal level of some of the foregoing views about emotional functioning in families. Like the family system, the social system maintains a balance between individuality and togetherness. In the face of increasing social anxiety, e.g., the prospect of war or economic depression, an imbalance in the direction of fusion, or indifferentiation, has been created in most societies. Like parents in an anxiety-ridden family, the society alternates between being overly permissive and overly harsh, overly involved in the lives of citizens or overly remote and uncaring. One outcome that can be expected, in Bowen's view, is that intensely fused, anxiety-laden subgroups may develop in society and begin to fight among themselves. Since the swing in our society appears to be away from an optimum balance of forces, the societal outlook does not appear favorable in Bowen's view.

FAMILY SYSTEMS THERAPY.

Goals of Therapy

The primary goal of Family Systems Therapy is for each family member to become disengaged from the *undifferentiated family ego mass* and to thereby achieve differentiation of self. If the therapist can help one member to achieve this, others will soon follow and the entire family can be un-fused and moved to a state of optimum balance (or at least a more favorable balance) of individuality and togetherness.

A second goal of therapy is reduction of anxiety in the family emotional field. The two goals are interdependent, however, and as the family becomes disengaged, anxiety will be lowered; if anxiety is low, differentiation becomes less important.

A third goal (remembering the multigenerational transmission process) is to disengage each partner's self from his or her family of origin whenever this appears to be a problem. Differentiation from the original fused family system makes it more likely that a spouse can become a self in his or her immediate family. Recall that cut-off from the family is never a real solution, but contact must be maintained or re-established along with an understanding of the emotional forces that created the cut-off in the first place. Disengagement without emotional distancing can then become an outcome of therapy.

Techniques of Therapy.

In the therapeutic setting, Bowen usually works with three persons—a triangle composed of two adults and himself as therapist. He intentionally omits using a child as a point of the triangle, even though the child may be the identified patient in the family, because he believes that the family problem is always between spouses, and the child's problems are simply symptoms of the couple's dysfunctional emotional system.

By the same token, Bowen does not work directly with the presenting problem, e.g., alcoholism or delinquency, because he sees these also as symptoms of emotional processes going on in the system. As the goals of disengagement and anxiety reduction are met, such symptoms, he believes, will diminish.

Bowen feels strongly that the therapist should not become involved in the family emotional system, but should remain disengaged from the system.

In working with a couple, Bowen usually addresses questions to one partner at a time and that partner responds directly to him. Rarely are the partners encouraged to interact with one another. The kinds of questions asked depends on the nature of the particular clinical situation; therapy with a couple will probably focus on nuclear family relationships, while work with an individual member may focus on the family of origin of each partner (Kerr, 1981, p. 257).

Summary

This chapter has reviewed the work of Murray Bowen—his Family Systems Theory and his therapy. Coming from a psychoanalytic background, Bowen moved from the study of the mother-patient symbiosis as an etiological factor in schizophrenia, to the conviction that the whole family is involved in pathology. His theory includes eight interlocking concepts: triangles, nuclear family emotional process, differentiation of self, multigenerational transmission process, emotional cutoff, sibling position, and societal emotional process. Central to all of these concepts are the two inter-related variables of (1) the individual's level of differentiation, and (2) the amount of anxiety in the emotional field. The goals of Bowen's therapy follow from the above variables: disengagement of the patient from his/her undifferentiated family ego mass, and reduction of anxiety in the family emotional field.

CHAPTER 11

Salvador Minuchin's Structural Family Therapy

BACKGROUND

Salvador Minuchin is a pioneer in family therapy who has made major contributions to both therapy and theory. Perhaps more than any other family theorist, Minuchin is committed to a general systems view, showing particular interest in homeostasis, feedback, system boundaries, subsystems, open and closed system properties, and other such features discussed in earlier chapters. In keeping with a system view, his therapy is also holistic, viewing individual behaviors as indicators of total family structure, and rejecting a linear view of causality in favor of a transactional view.

Minuchin, born in 1921, received traditional psychiatric training in Argentina. After completing a residency in child psychiatry in the United States, he went to Israel to fight in the 1948 War of Independence and, after the war, returned to the United States, where he became a fellow in child psychiatry with the Jewish Board of Guardians. After three years, he became director of the Wiltwyck School for Boys in New York, whose student body was largely made up of delinquent youngsters from black and Puerto Rican ghettos, a group at that time not customarily treated by the psychiatric community. Because traditional therapy was largely ineffective with these boys (as soon as they returned home, their delinquent behavior resumed), Minuchin began to suppose that something about their families was contributing to their continuing delinquency. This was the impetus for his developing a new approach for working with families. Introduced in the early 1960s as "conflict resolution therapy," it later came to be called "structural family therapy." The book *Families of the Slums* (Minuchin, Montalvo, Guerney, Rosman, & Schumer, 1967) grew out of his work at Wiltwyck and marked the first public presentation of structural therapy.

In 1965 Minuchin assumed the directorship of the Philadelphia Child Guidance Clinic, where he continued to work in the black ghetto. Originally a small clinic with a staff of 10, it eventually became the largest facility of its kind known, with a staff of 225 members (Goldenberg & Goldenberg, 1980, p. 179). Also associated with this clinic was the development of the view of psychosomatic illness as a symptom brought on and maintained by family structure. His therapeutic techniques have produced unusual success in treating diabetes, asthma, and anorexia nervosa—diseases largely resistant to other forms of psychotherapy.

Although he was traditionally trained in psychiatry, Minuchin is only minimally concerned with helping families achieve insight into or understanding of their problems, nor is he concerned with *growth* in the usual therapeutic sense; instead, emphasis in structural therapy is on the immediacy of a patient's reality. Focus of therapy is on the problems the family brings to therapy, the contextual setting of the family, and on problem-solving. Family problems are seen as originating in and sustained by family structures, and emphasis is always on active interventions aimed at *re-ordering* the family structure in order to bring about problem solution.

STRUCTURAL THEORY

The theoretical foundations of this model rest on the belief that "the whole and the parts can be properly examined only in terms of the relations that exist between the parts" (Aponte & Van Deusen, 1981, p. 311). Therapeutic techniques are therefore aimed at restructuring the internal organization of families and the linkages between components.

The structural dimensions most important to this theory are boundary, alignment, and power. *Boundary*, as Minuchin defines it, refers to the rules governing activities between members—who participates with whom, and how—as well as each member's activities with persons outside the family. Primary concern is with subsystem boundaries, which must be well-defined enough for members to carry out their functions without undue interference and still permit inter-action with other subsystems (Walsh, 1982, p. 12). *Alignment* includes both coalitions (joint action of two members against a third) and alliances (two who share a common interest that the third does not share). *Power*, the relative influence of each member on the outcome of an activity, determines who will prevail when there is parental disagreement. All of these structural dimensions have the potential for dysfunction.

Dysfunctions related to boundaries include the concepts of *enmeshment* and *disengagement*, and can be described along two dimensions of permeability and rigidity. Relatively imper-meable and rigid internal subsystem boundaries are asso-ciated with the disengaged system, and fluid, undifferentiated boundaries are characteristic of the enmeshed system. In an enmeshed family, differences among members are blurred, autonomy is interfered with, and the system may be unable to adapt and change. In a disengaged family impermeable boundaries keep members separate, and autonomy is achiev-ed at the expense of connectedness.

Dysfunctions associated with the dimension of alignment are (1) stable coalitions, (2) triangulation, and (3) detouring coalitions. In *stable coalitions*, members join together against another member in a rigid way that becomes a fixed characteristic of their ongoing relationship. In *triangulation*, each of two opposing parties seeks to joining with a third party against the other, with the third party vacillating, joining with first one and then the other. The *detouring coalition* is a form of stable coalition in which members attempt to reduce stress by designating a member as the source of the family problem and attacking that member.

Dysfunctions with regard to power grow out of a lack of functional power in the system; that is, members are not able to exercise the force necessary to carry out their appropriate functions. This may include weak *executive functioning*, where parents lack the power to direct their children, or *inhibition of developmental potential*, when individuals do not function in ways appropriate to their age (Aponte & Van Deusen, 1981, p. 315).

STRUCTURAL THERAPY

When interviewed by *Psychology Today* (Marcus, 1977), Minuchin was asked by the interviewer to describe for the reading public exactly what structural therapy is. The following clarifying exchange occurred between Minuchin and Mary Marcus:

> *Minuchin*: The structural approach to families as-
> sumes that a family is more than the individual psycho-
> dynamics of its members. A family runs by unstated rules
> that all the members understand. The implicit rules
> determine how, when, and to whom each of the family
> members relates. The sum of the rules or patterns of
> interaction is what I call the structure of the family. The
> structure organizes each person's behavior and his or her
> experience of reality. After a while, we are harnessed by our
> patterns of interaction. They prevent other types of en-

counter with life and with people. We have other possible ways of responding but we don't use them

Marcus: Can you give us an example of the way in which an implicit pattern governs events within a family?

Minuchin: For instance, in a family with an adolescent daughter who comes home late, experiments with drugs, is promiscuous, and doesn't obey rules at home, the father wants to impose a curfew. The daughter complains about his control, and the wife criticizes his rigid methods of discipline. The father withdraws. The mother implores the girl to behave, the daughter complains about her intrusiveness, and the father criticizes the mother's ineffectiveness. The mother withdraws. The daughter continues to misbehave. And the cycle continues.

Marcus: They probably can't see themselves behaving in any other way.

Minuchin: They cannot. Family patterns put blinders on people. On all of us. You are who you are in your context...

ASSESSMENT

Structural therapists do not "do" assessment in the usual sense, with diagnostic interviews or assessment instruments, but start immediately with the process of therapy. However, assessment in one sense is done in early stages of therapy when the therapist starts to identify the problem and to determine what family structures sustain it.

GOALS OF THERAPY

The goals of structural therapy are twofold: (1) to change the family organization, thereby changing functions, and (2) to solve family problems. To accomplish these goals, interventions are direct, concrete and action-oriented, intended to confront and challenge the family. Therapy is short-term, usually not longer than six months.

INTERVIEW PROCESS

The therapist may begin to work with a whole family in *joint* interview (this includes all who are involved in the problem). Later she/he may move to a *concurrent* process involving different subgroups in the same family, or use a sequential process in cases where an issue must be resolved with one subgroup before therapy can move on to the whole family. Various subgroup issues may be resolved sequentially before the whole family is reassembled. Whenever subgroup work is done, either concurrent or sequential, the therapist usually will call the entire family back for periodic sessions.

THERAPEUTIC INTERVENTIONS

The therapist never assumes a structurally neutral position, but is always actively organizing the interaction to meet structural goals and create change. In selecting interventions to use, the therapist may create two different sorts of interaction: one encourages interaction among family members, but the therapist does not enter into the discussion; instead she/he acts as observer, evaluator, or commentator. This is called *facilitating engagement*. The other kind of interaction, *centralizing engagement*, promotes interaction between family members and the therapist. In other words, the therapist can participate from inside the system, or can observe and comment from outside the system, depending on what needs to be restructured at any given time.

Structural therapy interventions fall under four divisions: *disassembly*, *construction*, *reinforcement*, and *reorganization*. To disassemble a structural pattern is simply to break it down. To construct a structural pattern is to develop structures either new to the system or underdeveloped in the system. To reinforce structure is to act to help maintain what exists or to amplify the scope and/or strength. To reorganize relations structurally is to rearrange patterns in a particular problem area along lines that are already accessible to the system, often in other areas of functioning (Aponte & Van Deusen, 1981, p. 335). Within this general framework are a great number of specific intervention techniques, which are often used in conjunction with behavior modification techniques and strategic therapy techniques.

Summary of "Treatment of Troubled Families"

Part 4 reviewed four models of clinical practice that take a system view in treating troubled families. The interactional view, growing out of the work of Gregory Bateson and the Mental Research Institute, draws from communication theory, cybernetic theory, and a variety of other influences. It is system-based, pragmatic, and focused on family interaction; its goal is to bring about second-order change in the family system.

The strategic therapy of Jay Haley is active, directive, and—some say—manipulative, with focus on the presenting problem as well as on dysfunctional relationships that are evidenced in rigid communication patterns and struggles for control in the relationships. Its dual goals are to change behavior of the identified patient and to change the system by creating disequilibrium within it.

Murray Bowen's therapy is based on a fully developed

Family Systems Theory that relies on the interrelated variables of differentiation and anxiety in the family emotional field. The goal of Family Systems Therapy is to help each member achieve differentiation from the family ego mass, to reduce anxiety in the family emotional field, and when needed, to disengage each member from his or her merged family of origin.

Salvador Minuchin's structural family therapy is based on the premise that all functioning grows out of the structure of the system; therefore, change in the family's structure creates change in family functioning. This is the first principle of structural therapy as well as its primary curative factor.

Despite differences in theory, practice, and goals of the models reviewed in this chapter, certain similarities are evident. Each is a true systems approach in that it looks to dysfunction in the total family as the source of problems, rather than looking for individual intrapsychic disturbance. Each sees the necessity for therapeutic intervention to interrupt positive feedback loops, and to disturb the homeostatic balance, thus forcing change in the system. Each emphasizes communication, either at a skill level, as does Satir, or as a reflection of structural features, as does Minuchin, or as a device for controlling the relationships in the system, as does Haley. Minuchin, like Bowen, believes that healthy family functioning is a matter of balance between belonging and independence, that clear boundaries between parent and child subsystems are essential, and that families who achieve a balance in relationships are healthier than those that are too close or too separated. Significantly, in all these models, we again see emphasis being placed on the bipolar dimensions of involvement and flexibility, with the extremes of overinvolvement-underinvolvement and rigidity-overflexibility being associated with dysfunctional family systems.

REFERENCES

Aponte, H. J., & Van Deusen, J. M. 1981. Structural family therapy. In Gurman, A. S., & Kniskern, D. P. (Eds.), *Handbook of Family Therapy*, pp. 310–360. New York: Brunner/Mazel.

Barton, C., & Alexander, J. F. (1981). Functional family therapy. In Gurman, A. S., & Kniskern, D. P. (Eds.), *Handbook of Family Therapy*, pp. 403–443. New York: Brunner/Mazel.

Bateson, G., Jackson, D., Haley, J., & Weakland, J. (1956). Toward a theory of schizophrenia. *Behavioral Science, 1*, 251–264.

Bowen, M. (1965). Family psychotherapy with schizophrenia in the hosptial and in private practice. In Boszormenyi-Nagy, I., & Framo, J. (Eds.), *Intensive Family Therapy*, pp. 213–243. Hagerstown, MD: Harper.

Bowen, M. (1975). Family therapy after twenty years. In Arieti, S., Freeman, D. X., & Dyrud, J. E. (Eds.), *American Handbook of Psychology*. V. *Treatment* (2nd ed.), pp. 369–379. New York: Basic Books.

Bowen, M. (1978). *Family Therapy in Clinical Practice*. New York: Gardner Press.

Fisch, R., Watzlawick, P., Weakland, J., & Bodin, J. (1977). On becoming a family therapist. In Watzlawick, P., & Weakland, J. (Eds.), *The Interactional View*, pp. 308–324. New York: Norton.

Fox, R. E. (1976). Family therapy. In Weiner, I. B. (Ed.), *Clinical Methods in Psychology*, pp. 452–515. New York: Wiley.

Goldenberg, I., & Goldenberg, H. (1980). *Family Therapy: An Overview*. Monterey, CA: Brooks/Cole.

Gurman, A. S., & Kniskern, D. P. (1981). *Handbook of Family Therapy*. New York: Brunner/Mazel.

Haley, J. (1973). *Uncommon Therapy*. New York: Norton.

Haley, J. (1976). *Problem-Solving Therapy*. New York: Harper.

Haley, J., & Hoffman, L. (1967). *Techniques of Family Therapy*. New York: Basic Books.

Kerr, M. E. (1981). Family systems theory and therapy. In Gurman, A. S., & Kniskern, D. P. (Eds.), *Handbook of Family Therapy*, pp. 226–264. New York: Brunner/Mazel.

Laing, R. D. (1961): *Self and Others*. New York: Pantheon.

Madanes, C. (1984). *Behind the One-Way Mirror: Advances in the Practice of Strategic Therapy*. San Francisco: Jossey-Bass.

Marcus, M. (1977, January). The artificial boundary between self and family. *Psychology Today*, 66–72.

Minuchin, S., Montalvo, B., Guerney, G., Rosman., & Schumer, F. (1967). *Families of the Slums*. New York: Basic Books.

Walsh, F. (Ed.) (1982). *Normal Family Processes*. New York: Guilford Press.

Watzlawick, P. (1978). *The Language of Change*. New York: Basic Books.

Watzlawick, P., Beavin, J. H., & Jackson, D. D. (1967). *Pragmatics of Human Communication*. New York: Norton.

Watzlawick, P., Weakland, J. H., & Fisch, R. (1974). *Change: Principles of Problem Formation and Problem Resolution*. New York: Norton.

Weakland, J. H. (1981). One thing leads to another. In Wilder-Mott, C., & Weakland, J. H. (Eds.), *Rigor and Imagination: Essays from the Legacy of Gregory Bateson*. New York: Praeger.

Weakland, J. H., Fisch, R., Watzlawick, P., & Bodin, A. M. (1974). Brief therapy: Focused problem resolution. *Family Process, 13,* 141–168.
Wilder-Mott, C., & Weakland, J. H. (Eds.) (1981). *Rigor & Imagination: Essays from the Legacy of Gregory Bateson.* New York: Praeger.

PART V

FAMILY REPONSE: CONFIRMING AND DISCONFIRMING STYLES

Confirmation:
Concept and Components

Despite differences in vocabulary, there seems to be rather general agreement that certain kinds of family interaction are associated with troubled families in which children grow up with lowered self-esteem, spouses exhaust themselves in futile and frustrating struggles, and members feel misunderstood, trapped, isolated, insignificant, confused, or unreal.

About the other side of the coin—how families interact when they are untroubled or "normal"—there is less knowledge and even less agreement. We can start, however, by assuming that family interaction has the potential for providing support and concern not otherwise available. It can create feelings of individual self-worth; it can allow members to share their deepest emotional experiences, and it can enhance their sense of reality and identity. Compared to an outside world that is often cold and abrasive, the family can provide comfort, intimacy and the assurance of unquestioning acceptance from others. The unfortunate truth seems to be that families live up to this potential only rarely, more often being a source of major personal and interpersonal problems of members.

While up to this point families have been described in rather general terms, dealing primarily with theoretical material, this part will be more explicit in describing how families behave—how they *sound* and appear to observers—in order to see more precisely what it means for a family to be identified as open or closed, functional or dysfunctional, healthy or unhealthy, rigid or flexible, enmeshed or disengaged. To do this, we will be examining an variety of response tactics, which, to make them more manageable, have been grouped as *confirming responses* and *disconfirming responses*. With the limited amount of available research data, it appears that confirming tactics are likely to be used in flexible open-family systems, in functional families, and in families with an optimal mix of intimacy and autonomy, while disconfirming response tactics are more commonly observed and reported in inflexible, closed, or disordered family systems, where people have difficulty making meaning together, and in which relationships are unsatisfactory and sometimes seriously disturbed.

It is the purpose of this chapter and of Chapter 13 to lay the foundation for a tentative classification of families in Chapter 14 according to their confirming or disconfirming styles of response. In this, we are mindful of Haley's (1967) admonition that "a proper classification system for families should be based upon types of interactions in families, rather than characteristics of individual members" (p. 78).

THE CONCEPT OF CONFIRMATION

The use of the terms "confirmation" and "disconfirmation" is not original here or even original with the behavioral sciences, having appeared for several decades in philosophical and religious literature, most importantly in the writings of theologian Martin Buber. In recent years, confirmation has begun to receive attention in the psychiatric and communication literature and has been the subject of limited empirical research.

As used by Buber, confirmation described a significant feature of all human interaction—perhaps the *most* significant. Buber (1957) attributed broad existential importance to the act of confirming another, calling it "the measurement of the humanness of a society" and asserting that the disuse of the capacity to confirm is "the real weakness and questionableness of the human race" (p. 110). Further stressing the effects of confirmation at all levels of human existence, Buber wrote:

> The basis of man's life with man in twofold, and it is one—
> the wish of every man to be confirmed as what he is ... and
> the innate capacity in man to confirm his fellow man in
> this way. (p. 102)

According to Buber, man, alone of all animals, *becomes* what he is through interaction with other humans; therefore he needs constant recognition from them in order to experience his own identity. Deprived of such recognition, man becomes doubtful of his own experience in the world and unsure of his own identity as a human. This, is essence, is what is meant by confirmation: whatever actions on the part of a person that cause another to feel recognized, acknowledged, and endorsed (Laing, 1961, pp. 89–90).

Confirmation first requires simple recognition of another's presence and existence, but beyond that, it implies a recognition of the other's humanness, as contrasted to the treatment of him as a *thing*, a stereotype or an object in the environment. This aspect of confirmation was made somewhat more explicit by the existential psychologist James F. T. Bugental, who associated confirmation with encounter, engagement, and dialogue—all existential terms for describing relationships between persons. Bugental (1965) wrote:

> Genuine encounter is the coming together of people who
> recognize the be-ing-ness of themselves and each other.

> Buber has contrasted the "I-it" relationship with the "I-Thou" relationship. When I meet you and regard you as an object rather than as another subject, I give you the status of a thing rather than a be-ing. This is an "I-it" relationship. It is not a genuine encounter. When I meet you and recognize you as another be-ing, this is an "I-Thou" relationship and is an encounter. This process of recognition of the other as be-ing in his own world is what is known as *confirmation.* (p. 29)

Implicit in Buber's description is the underlying idea that confirmation means acceptance of the other person as he/she is, as a unique individual, different, but no less real or acceptable—and our acceptance must be unconditional. Friedman (1985) elaborates on this point:

> We need to be confirmed in our uniqueness yet need to be confirmed by others who are different from us ....But other persons, including our parents, are not always willing to confirm us in our uniqueness. We cannot become ourselves without other people who call us to realize our created uniqueness in response to our life tasks. Many of us, unfortunately, have experienced "confirmation" of a very different nature, confirmation with strings attached. Many of us are, in effect, offered a contact which reads: "We will confirm you only if you will conform to our model of good child, the good churchgoer, the good student, the good citizen, the good soldier." (p. 197)

Confirmation has, in recent years, become recognized as essential for mental health, and disconfirmation has been associated with mental illness, especially with schizophrenia. R. D. Laing, a spokesman for the psychiatric point of view about confirmation, has described it as a process through which individuals are "endorsed" by others. Laing (1961) also expressed particular concern about *disconfirmation,* reporting that disconfirming interaction is a characteristic pattern that has emerged from his work with troubled families. In such families, Laing noted, one child is frequently singled out for especially destructive treatment from other members. As he describes it, the behavior of the family "does not so much involve a child who has been subjected to outright neglect or even to obvious trauma, but a child who has been subjected to subtle but persistent *disconfirmation,* usually unwittingly" (p. 82).

Whether chronic disconfirmation is limited to troubled families with recognized pathology (as Laing implies) is questionable. Friedman (1983) sees it as being even more widespread than this when he writes:

> To talk of confirmation of otherness in the family may seem a contradiction in terms in the face of the experience of countless persons the world over for whom the family has become little more than a forced grouping of people who do not like, much less love, one another. For many, perhaps most, people, the family is characterized by dominance and submission, ... bullying, manipulation, seduction, collusion, mystification, and chicanery. (p. 119)

Although confirmation has been identified as crucial in forming and maintaining any healthy human relationship, it has received most attention in clinical or therapeutic settings, particularly those where family treatment is conducted. Like earlier chapters, this chapter draws heavily on the work done at the Mental Research Institute in Palo Alto, by Boszormenyi-Nagy and Framo in Philadelphia, by Wynne and his associates in Bethesda, and by Gregory Bateson. Most importantly, this chapter makes use of Laing's work at Tavistock Institute in London. Based on the reported clinical experiences of these scholars in the area of family communication and family therapy, this chapter refines the concept of confirmation by identifying the general components of confirming and disconfirming response; in Chapter 13 these will be classified according to major groupings, and in Chapter 14, the groups of confirming and disconfirming response types will be related to a proposed typology of family systems.

THE COMPONENTS OF CONFIRMATION

Because the feeling of being confirmed or disconfirmed is a subjective experience, it is difficult to identify its behavioral components with great precision. Laing (1961), however, noted some of the more obvious modes:

> Modes of confirmation or disconfirmation vary. Confirmation could be through a responsive smile (visual) a handshake (tactile), an expression of sympathy (auditory). A confirmatory response is relevant to the evocative action, it accords recognition to the evocatory act, and accepts its significance for the evoker, if not for the respondent. A confirmatory reaction is a direct response, it is "to the point," on "the same wave-length" as the initiatory or evocatory action. (p. 82)

In Watzlawick, Beavin, and Jackson's (1967) important book about the pragmatics of human communication, the authors acknowledge the contributions of both Buber and Laing to the development of the concept of confirmation, and themselves describe confirmation as a subtle but powerful validation of one's self-image, which, if denied in interaction with others, can have severe emotional consequences. They described the confirmation of a person's self-image as "probably the greatest single factor ensuring mental development and stability that has so far emerged from our study of communication" (p. 84).

The descriptive material provided by Watzlawick, et al. (1967) to illustrate disconfirmation includes instances of total unawareness of another person, lack of accurate perception of the other's point of view, and deliberate distortion or denial of the other's self-attributions. According to their interpretation, however, disconfirmation is somewhat more than a simple denial of another's self-image; it also goes beyond accepting or rejecting the content of what the other says. As they describe it,

> confirmation ... is no longer concerned with the truth or falsity—if there be such a criteria—of P's definition of himself, but rather negates the reality of P as the source of such a definition. In other words, while rejection amounts

to the message "you are wrong," disconfirmation says in effect, "you do not exist." (p. 86)

Thus, in the few direct allusions to confirming response, several distinct elements are mentioned. That is, response is called confirming to the extent that it performs the following functions:

(1) it expresses recognition of the other person's existence.

(2) it acknowledges the other person as a unique being-in-relation, rather than simply as an object in the environment.

(3) it expresses awareness of the significance (or worth) of the other.

(4) it endorses the other's self-experience as he/she expresses it.

In an effort to be more specific about what particular behaviors are likely to be confirming or disconfirming, it should be noted that it is never possible to point with absolute certainty to special acts that universally perform confirming or disconfirming functions for all people. As we have already seen, individuals differ widely in the way they *interpret* the same acts toward them, so in attempting to understand the dynamics of confirmation, we must remind ourselves that human beings largely create their own emotional pleasure and pain in any experience. We do not always react consistently to any given stimulus as a "signal response," but interpret the stimuli we encounter and assign meaning to them (Mead, 1934). Along with other interpretations, we define and evaluate ourselves by observing others' reactions to us. That is, we define the total situation in some way, and our definition always includes the assignment of attitudes toward us on the part of others present.

Despite considerable variation in each person's interpretation of how others feel about him or her, certain acts *do* serve as rather consistent cues, and are generally accepted by most persons as reflecting specific attitudes toward them. Thus these behaviors, verbal and nonverbal, have message value and are able to arouse in the receiver feelings of being real or unreal, accepted or rejected, valued or scorned, understood or misunderstood, human or objectified. It is these specific acts and their customary interpretation that will be the subject of the following chapter.

CHAPTER 13

Confirming and Disconfirming Response in Families

DISCONFIRMING RESPONSE

A number of specific response behaviors (verbal and nonverbal) have been described by clinicians and theorists as being damaging to the self-view of a receiver in an interaction. These are grouped here into three broad categories, each representing a somewhat different "style" of response, although the groups are not mutually exclusive. These categories are: (1) indifferent response, (2) impervious response, and (3) disqualifying response. Each of these has the power to disconfirm because it denies one or more of the components of confirmation mentioned in Chapter 12; that is, it denies another's existence, it denies relatedness between speakers, it rejects the attempt to communicate, it questions the other's

perception or self-experience, or it denies the other's significance. Each category will be examined in this chapter.

Disconfirming by Indifference

To deny another's existence/(or presence) is to deny the
most fundamental acceptance of him/her. Indifference need
not be total, however, to be disconfirming; it may simply imply
a rejection of the other's attempt to relate or to communicate.
These aspects are treated separately here, although in reality
there is much overlap.

Denial of Presence

Confirmation of a person begins with awareness of his/her
existence. The appearance of unawareness is disconfirming
because it denies *all* aspects of the self-view: no reality, no
relatedness, no validity of experience, no significance,
uniqueness, or worth. Further, that person then becomes a
depersonalized thing, not a feeling human being. Such
indifferent treatment is devastating to a person of any age, but
is especially terrifying for a child, as social critic Leontine
Young (1965) noted:

> Adults fear death. Children fear annihilation. The two may
> seem to come to much the same thing in the end but if so,
> the fear of a child comes to overshadow and perhaps to
> merge with the fear of the adult. They are, with all their
> similarity, quite different things ....When a little child is
> neither seen nor heard, he begins shortly to be frightened.
> There is no way for him to know that he is there except as
> he sees himself reflected in the eyes of others. For a time he
> can be alone, engrossed in some special interest ... but if
> the solitude outlasts the interest, alarm begins to mount. ...
> He is not afraid of being killed, *he is afraid of being erased.*
> (pp. 68–69)

Because any attention at all, even negative attention in the
form of punishment, is preferable to the fear of non-being, a
child, as we have seen before, may engage in the most
outrageous behavior in order to avoid "erasure." In a similar

vein, psychiatrist Eric Berne (1964) wrote about the human need for "stroking," a term he employed to denote any act implying recognition of another's presence. Positive strokes are generally preferred in the form of an "approving audience," but even negative strokes in the form of disapproval are better than no strokes at all. Similarly, in the family, even unpleasant or critical talk seems to be preferable to the absence of talk. Even when the content of the talk is of little consequence, is ritualistic or even meaningless, the very act of talking to a person is sufficient to reassure that person that he or she exists. Any talk at all, therefore, qualifies as being somewhat confirming.

The absence of even a minimal show of recognition has been associated with alienation, self-destructiveness, violence against others, and psychosis. Laing (1961) used the case of "Peter," a psychotic patient of 25, to illustrate the possible long-term effects of chronic indifference toward a child, who may, as a consequence, come to believe that he has no presence at all—or to feel guilty that he *does*, feeling that he has no right to even occupy space:

> Peter . . . was a young man who was preoccupied with guilt *because* he occupied a place in the world, even in a physical sense. He could not realize, make real to himself, that he had a right to have any presence for others . . . . A peculiar aspect of his childhood was that his presence in the world was largely ignored. No weight was given to the fact that he was in the same room while his parents had intercourse. He had been physically cared for in that he had been fed and kept warm, and underwent no physical separation from his parents during his earlier years. Yet he had been consistently treated as though he did not "really" exist. Perhaps worse than the experience of physical separation was to be in the same room as his parents and ignored, not malevolently, but through sheer indifference. (p. 119)

Recalling the infant's powerful need for physical contact, the child's need for approval, the juvenile's need for group acceptance, and the various adult needs that all require recognition as a base, it is not difficult to see that the total indifference that suggests the metamessage "you do not exist" is probably the most devastating form of disconfirmation.

A response that suggests indifference includes various behaviors (but are not limited to these): looking away from the other when he or she is speaking, avoiding eye contact, interrupting or "talking over" the other, turning to speak with a third person while the other is still talking, interjecting comments that are irrelevant, engaging in other activities while talking (reading or television watching, as common examples), simply leaving the field while the other is still talking, and, of course, silence when a response seems expected or required. Each of these acts suggests, if not absolute indifference, at least an unwillingness to validate the other by giving him/her undivided attention, or even by acknowledging his/her presence.

Denial of Involvement

Extreme instances of disconfirmation like that of "Peter" are presumed to be rare because even the slightest attention at least confirms one's existence and presence. Lesser shows of indifference, however, are common and still create feelings of alienation, frustration, and lowered self-worth. Although basic recognition is a necessary first step in confirming another, it is not in itself sufficient unless accompanied by some further indication of a willingness to be involved—to relate to the other *as a person* rather than as an object in the environment.

The precise behaviors by which one person indicates to another that he/she is interested in relating are not fully known, but rather clear indications of *unwillingness* to be involved have emerged from research. These include both verbal and nonverbal indicators that appear to evoke in the receiver the metamessage, "I do not wish to relate to you."

Language has an enormous, largely unexplored power to erect barriers between people. We know, for example, that the habitual use of impersonal constructions that *avoid* first-person references (I, me, my, or mine) is characteristic of persons who resist involvement ("affiliation") with others (Lorenz, 1955; Will, 1959; Bateson, 1960). Such avoidance of personal reference may take the form of reliance on the collective "we" or "you" when a speaker is actually referring only to himself/herself, or the tendency to begin sentences with "there," as "There seems to be . . . .," when making what appears to be a personal statement. Carl Rogers (1959) noted once that his more rigid patients—those who had difficulty in relating—would almost never say, "I feel . . . ," "I believe . . . ," or "I am uncertain about . . . ," preferring to substitute something like "There are . . . ," "the situation seems to be . . . ," or "they say that . . . " (p. 104).

The reliance of speaker on impersonal language constructions clearly restricts his or her ability to disclose personal feelings to others. The importance of self-disclosure, openness, and genuine emotional expression are popular themes in much psychological literature and need no support here. Strong arguments for the value of revealing the "present and particular being" (to use Buber's words) have been advanced by many humanistic writers besides Rogers—among them, Sidney Jourard, Abraham Maslow, and Erich Fromm.

An entire family may adopt an impersonal style of interacting through family rules that inhibit the genuine expression of feelings, substituting instead clichés, ritual interaction, or intellectualized forms of address. John Powell (1969) eloquently describes the possible consequences when a family habitually inhibits "feeling" expression among its members:

> If I really want you to know who I am, I must tell you about my stomach (gut-level) as well as my head. My ideas, judgements and decisions are quite conventional . . . but the *feelings* that lie under my ideas, judgements, and convictions are uniquely mine. . . . Most of us feel that others will not tolerate such emotional honesty in communication. We would rather defend our dishonesty on the grounds that it might hurt others, and, having rationalized our phoniness into nobility, we settle for superficial relationships. This occurs not only in the cases of casual acquaintances, but even with members of our own families; it destroys authentic communication within marriages. Consequently we ourselves do not grow, nor do we help anyone else to grow. Meanwhile we have to live with repressed emotions—a dangerous and self-destructive path to follow. Any relationship which is to have the nature

of true personal encounter must be based on this honest, open, gut-level communication. The alternative is to remain in my prison, to endure inch-by-inch death as a person. (p. 55)

The free and open disclosure of one's feelings to another invites the other to do the same and suggests a willingness to be personally involved with him. By the same token, family interaction styles that inhibit personal expression implicitly deny member involvement with one another fostering fragmentation of the system and alienation of members from one another.

Other strong indicators of a person's wish to remain uninvolved are found in his or her nonverbal behavior, particularly in eye contact. Research has consistently shown that those persons who prefer intimacy to distance are likely to look directly at others while speaking with them, but that "low affiliation" persons—those who resist intimacy—tend to focus their eyes elsewhere. One team of researchers (Exline, Gray, & Schuette, 1965), in reporting the results of their investigation of the relationship between eye contact and intimacy, concluded:

In general, a continued exchange of glances would seem to signal a willingness or a desire to become involved with one another, or to maintain an ongoing interaction. Avoidance, on the other hand, would seem to indicate a lack of interest in initiating a relationship, or in the case of an ongoing interaction, would indicate that one or more parties wishes to break away. (p. 202)

Clearly, for most people, interaction with a person who avoids eye contact tends to evoke the metamessage, "I do not wish to relate to you."

Directly relevant to the subject of disconfirmation is an experimental study (Jacobs, 1973), which found that subjects reported feeling *most* disconfirmed when exposed to a condition (role-played) in which the other speaker turned away from them, avoided eye contact, made no facial response (such as smiling or nodding), and performed other unrelated tasks while they were speaking. Although such "distancing" behaviors are somewhat understandable in the case of persons who are strangers or newly met (as in the Jacobs study), it is puzzling to find a high incidence of like behaviors reported in families, where presumed *intimates* also engaged in unrelated activities while conversing. That is, they turned away from one another, avoided eye contact, carried on conversations from different rooms of the house, and otherwise withheld involvement (Stachowiak, 1970).

Denial of Communication: Irrelevance and Monologue

Even when a person's existence is recognized and the relationship acknowledged, disconfirmation can still occur when the quality of the response is such that it denies the other's attempt to communicate and arouses the metamessage, "We are not communicating." This aspect of indifferenct response includes behaviors ranging from mildly irritating to severely pathogenic.

Totally irrelevant response is much like denial of presence in that the person whose conversation is repeatedly ignored may soon come to doubt his or her very existence, and at best will feel that he or she is not heard, not attended to, or not regarded as significant. Perhaps for this reason Laing (1961) called *relevance* the "crux of confirmation," noting that only by responding relevantly can one lead significance to another's communication and accord him recognition (p. 82).

Probably the most potent form of communication denial is *monologue*, in which one speaker continues on and on with whatever he or she has to say, neither hearing nor acknowledging anything the other person says or tries to interject. Monologue reflects unawareness and/or unconcern about the other expect as a socially acceptable audience for the speaker's own self-listening. Brown and Keller (1973) comment on this phenomenon:

> Communication marked by indifference for the other person results in a speech in which the intended receiver is the self. The other person serves almost exclusively as a stimulant. Just as an amputated leg or arm can be experienced as a phantom limb, so another person can be experienced as a part of one's own communication system—a kind of phantom. And this is what happens in

monologue, a kind of communication we learn early in life. (p. 91)

Sometimes the monologist pauses long enough to permit the other to speak, but then continues without acknowledgment of anything the other may have said; sometimes it may even appear that the monologist is listening, but then he/she continues in such a way as to make it clear that his/her speech is simply a continuation of communication with himself/herself.

Disconfirming by Imperviousness

The term imperviousness, as used here, follows Laing's usage and refers to a peculiar unawareness of another's perceptions (Watzlawick, et al., 1967, p. 91). In the family context it can be described as a spiral, beginning with a parent's denial of a child's perceptions and feelings, followed by the child's failure to understand that his/her perceptions have been misperceived or deliberately distorted. The spiral usually starts because the parent fears that the child's feelings are not what the child *should be* feeling. When parents feel threatened or embarrassed by their child's "undesirable" feelings, they may respond by simply denying that the child feels as he/she reports it. The child, in turn, may not recognize the maneuver and becomes confused as to what he/she really *does* feel or experience.

Imperviousness can take a variety of forms that will be discussed in this section: denial, attribution, and reinterpretation; pseudo-confirmation; selective confirmation; substitution; and the evoking of rights and obligations.

Distortion, Attribution, and Reinterpretation

Imperviousness to another's real perceptions or feelings is disconfirming because it questions the validity of personal experience and reduces feelings of autonomy. Instead of accepting the other's self-description as accurate, the impervious responder engages in various tactics that tend to negate or discredit the other's expression. This may take the form of denying that the other *has* such a feeling ("I know you don't mean that"; "you don't really feel that way") or it may involve reinterpretation of the expressed feeling in a more acceptable way, substituting some preferred feeling of the responder, or challenging the speaker's right to have such a feeling. We saw in Chapter 7 how imperviousness in a severely pathological form was used to mystify "Ruby" by making her feel that she was crazy because she *correctly* perceived her family's dislike of her. Here are other examples to help clarify the concept.

In using denial and reinterpretation of affect, the responder may hear and understand what the speaker says, but responds by going beyond what has been said to explain *why* the speaker doesn't feel as he or she says. Consider, for example, the small child who, in a moment of rage, screams, "I hate you!" to his mother. The mother's interpretive response might be, "Of course you don't hate your mother; you're only saying that because you're tired and need your nap." In a similar way, a husband who is confronted with unwanted emotionality on the part of his wife may deny that her tears have any validity and dismiss them with, "You're only upset because it's time for your period." Or consider the family fight in which one member's expression is rejected on the grounds that "You're only saying that to make me mad"—implying that the responder has some unusual access to the other's private, unspoken motivation. In the following exchange between a mother and daughter, the mother interprets the daughter's "unacceptable" feelings as an indication that the daughter is "ill."

> *Mother:* I don't blame you, dear, but I know your don't mean that.
> *Daughter:* But I do mean it!.
> *Mother:* Now, dear, I know you don't. I'm your mother. You can't help yourself.
> *Daughter:* I *can* help myself!
> *Mother:* You can't because you're ill. If I thought for a moment you weren't ill, I'd be furious (Laing, 1965, p. 363).

Denial is sometimes difficult to recognize at first glance because it may include socially approved behavior. For example, reassuring another or trying to reduce the other's self-doubt is often thought to be useful, appropriate, or even therapeutic behavior, unless we recognize that the self-experience of the other is still being questioned. Laing (1972) provided the following example of a fantasy conversation between a mother and her 14-year-old daughter:

> *Mother:* You are evil.
> *Daughter:* No, I'm not.
> *Mother:* Yes, you are.
> *Daughter:* Uncle Jack doesn't think so.
> *Mother:* He doesn't love you as I do. Only a mother really knows the truth about her daughter, and only one who loves you as I do will ever tell you the truth about yourself no matter what it is. If you don't believe me, just look at yourself in the mirror carefully and you will see that I'm telling the truth.
>
> The daughter did, and saw that her mother was right after all, and realized how wrong she had been not to be grateful for having a mother who so loved her that she would tell the truth about herself, whatever it might be.
>
> The above example may appear disturbing, even sinister. Suppose we changed one word in it: replace "evil" by "pretty." Now take another look:
>
> *Mother:* You are pretty.
> *Daughter:* No, I'm not.
> *Mother:* Yes you are.
> *Daughter:* Uncle Jack doesn't think so.
> *Mother:* He doesn't love you as I do. Only a mother really knows the truth about her daughter, and only the one who loves you as I do will ever tell you the truth about yourself no matter what it is. If you don't believe me, just look at yourself in the mirror carefully, and you will see that I'm telling you the truth.

About the above example, Laing (1972) comments:

> The *technique* is the same. Whether the attribution is pretty, good, beautiful, ugly, or evil, the *structure* is identical. The structure is so common that we hardly notice it unless the attribution jars. We all employ some recognizably similar version of this technique and may be prepared to justify it. I suggest that we reflect upon the *structure* of the *induction*, not only the content thereof (pp. 121–123).

Pseudoconfirmation

A somewhat different form of imperviousness occurs when a responder creates and bestows on another person an inaccurate identity, then confirms the false identity, although it is not a part of the other's self-experience at all. (We have already seem a similar dynamic at work when we discussed family projection process, internal dialogue, and family myth.) Thus, a mother who insists that her daughter is always obedient and "never any trouble at all" may be able to interpret her daughter's most rebellious aggression in a way that fits the placid image she holds of her daughter. And, as we saw in the last chapter, the pathological family myth can be supported with this device, so that the parents of even a murderous psychopath may describe their son as "a good boy." Such a false confirmation may endorse a fiction of what the other is wished to be, without any real recognition of what he or she really is or feels. It also appears in less pathological form as simply a well-meaning attempt to reassure someone who is distressed, as we saw in the mother-daughter exchange described earlier. Other common examples might be:

- Of course you're not afraid! No son of mine is a coward!
- Stop crying! You have absolutely nothing to cry about!
- How can you be so silly as to worry about a little thing like that!
- No matter what you say, I know you still love me.

Such responses constitute a deliberate rejection of the other person's "feeling" description and often a rejection of his or her basic identity, raising doubts about the validity of that person's way of experiencing by suggesting, "You don't really feel as you say you do; you are only *imagining* that you feel that way."

Selective Confirmation

Still another variation of imperviousness occurs when the speaker responds in a selective way, rewarding the other person with attention and relevant response only when he or she communicates in an approved fashion, but becoming indifferent if the other's speech or behavior does not meet with approval. This may mean that the responder limits responses to those topics personally initiated, but ignores any topic initiated by the other person. Typical of this tactic is the instance reported by Brodey (1959) of the mother who evoked smiles in her infant by tickling and playing with him, but who never responded to the infant's initial smiles at her (pp. 370–402). In a similar way, a parent may respond only to a conversation he or she initiates with a child, ignoring the child's talk when it is about a subject of the *child's* choosing. This kind of response affects a child's feeling of autonomy as well as his or her feeling of self-worth. It also seems related to the point made earlier that genuine dialogue requires alternation of subject and object roles—that one person's self-esteem may be choked off if he or she is constantly force-fed an object role in support of another person's subject role. The family member who is never rewarded for initiative or spontaneity will soon learn to play a perpetual object role opposite the other person, because that is the only role in which reinforcement is received. This form of imperviousness contributes to a feeling of being "thingafied," when a person is told how he feels, regardless of how *he* thinks he feels, when his talents and abilities are described without any data to support such a description, when motives are ascribed to him without any reference to his own experience of himself, when his own efforts at self-expression are ignored or discounted unless they match the false image held by the other person.

Substitution

This is a form of imperviousness that occurs when a responder denies another's expressed feeling and replaces it with something that is more descriptive of the responder's *own* wants or feelings. Laing uses the example of a child playing noisily in the evening when his mother is tired and would like to get to bed. A straight statement would be:
"I'm tired and want you to go to bed."
or
"Go to bed because I say so."
or
"Go to bed because it's your bedtime."

By contrast, a substitution would be:
"I know you're tired, darling, and want to go to bed now" (Laing, 1965, p. 345).

Symonds (1962) noted the same phenomenon in some parental communication with a child, calling it *externalization*, which occurs when a speaker asserts that something is true of the listener when it is really a part of the experience of the speaker himself (Symonds, 1962, pp. 98–101). For example, a wife may say to her husband, "You don't want to go to the movies tonight, do you?" (meaning "*I* don't want to go . . . ."). Externalization may also occur when an adult tells a child what the child *doesn't* want, as "You don't want to eat all that candy," or "You don't want to play in that dirty old mud." Such an admonition is impervious because the child in most cases *does* want to eat the candy and play in the mud, thus must choose between denying his or her own wishes or risking parental displeasure, so either choice becomes fearful.

Evoking Rights and Obligations

A common version of imperviousness is one in which the responder suggests that the first speaker has no *right* to feel as he says he does. Using again the example of the child who screams, "I hate you!" to his mother, her response to this might be, "Your should be ashamed to feel that way about your own mother!", or in reply to an adolescent's report of being miserable, the parent might respond, "How can you possibly be unhappy after all we've done for you?" In each of these examples, an element of guilt has been introduced, either regarding the existence of some undesired feeling, (hate, unhappiness) or the expression of it. This is especially powerful in psychologically enmeshed families because it implies that one member (usually a parent) has the right to determine how another member (usually a child) can experience himself or his world. This implication is, of course, incompatible with individual feelings of autonomy.

The consequences of imperviousness (under various different names) has received considerable attention in psychiatric writings. As we saw in the last chapter, Laing (1965) described "mystification," meaning the substitution of a speaker's motivation as a way of exploiting the other while expressing only benevolence. Boszormenyi-Nagy (1965) wrote of disturbed family interaction in which the "autonomous otherness" of certain family members is ignored when another members speaks *for* them, interpreting their motives and describing their feelings (p. 65). Friedman (1955) expressed it in somewhat more poetic terms when he wrote, "If we overlook the 'otherness' of the other person . . . we shall see him in our image and not as he really is in his concrete uniqueness" (p. 102).

Disconfirming by Disqualification

According to Watzlawick (1964), disqualification is a technique that enables one to say something without really saying it, to deny without really saying "no" and to disagree without really disagreeing (p. 18). Various forms of response are included in this broad category: (1) attack, blame, and disparagement, (2) unclear response, and (3) incongruenty. Although different in style, each shares the common feature of avoiding blame and arousing feelings of "wrongness" in the receiver. The metamessage, "I am not to blame," can be extended to, " . . . because it's somebody else's fault," or " . . . because I am not saying anything for which I can be held accountable."

Attack, Blame and Disparagement
In families were disqualification is the rule, any indication of approval of what another member says is rare, but direct messages of disapproval abound. A member seldom says, "I'm glad you said that," or "That makes me feel good," but members instead suggest, "You shouldn't have said that to me, in that particular way, or in this particular context." Haley, Sluzki, and other members of the Mental Research Institute, have made important contributions to our understanding of this response form. Haley (1959) describes how such family interaction sounds:

Typically, if one family member says something, another indicates it shouldn't have been said or wasn't said properly. If one criticizes the other, he is told that he misunderstands and should behave differently. If one compliments the other, he is told he doesn't do this often enough, or he has some ulterior purpose. Should a family member try to avoid communicating, the others will indicate this "passivity" is demanding and indicate he should initiate more. All family members may report they always feel they are in the wrong. However, they do not necessarily directly oppose each other or openly reject one another's statements. If one suggests going to a particular place, the other may not say "no," but rather is likely to indicate, "Why must we always go where you suggest?" Or the response may be the sigh of a brave martyr who must put up with this sort of thing. (p. 366)

Disqualification of this kind may also combine personal attack *and* disjunction of response. This occurs when a reply shifts attention from the content of the other person's message to some quality of the speaker, with the added suggestion that he or she is not to be relied on—too young, too old, too inexperienced, too stupid, or otherwise incompetent for his/her message to have validity. This combination creates an especially unanswerable put-down by evoking a strong metamessage of worthlessness:

"Can't you do *anything* right?"

"Why must you *always* ... ?"

"What do you know about it anyway?"

"Just shut up and keep out of this!"

The attack mode of disqualification is not usually so direct, however; rather, members fight their battles and defend themselves in devious ways, and messages are seldom what they appear. Hostility may be disguised as humor, punishment as benevolence, malicious acts as incidental or beyond the control of the perpetrator; criticism is claimed to be without critical intent, speakers constantly shift ground, denying that they meant what they said, claiming the other person must have misunderstood, or vacillating when confronted with opposition. A member may insist that something "dosen't matter," and then make it clear that it *did* matter; the injunction "don't worry," is the lead-in to messages intended to arouse worry; family members may insist that they "forgive and forget" another's misdoings, but endlessly repeat and discuss the "forgotten" episodes (Laing & Esterson, 1964, pp. 75–108). Under attack, a member may explain away a serious message as "only a joke." Children are trained to rely on "verbal magic" as a device for avoiding punishment, as by mouthing "I'm sorry" without any real contrition.

Unclear or Ambiguous Response

As we have seen, an unclear message may be used as a way of avoiding intimacy or involvement with another because it often generates the metamessage "We are not communicating," sometimes translated as "We are not relating." Here we will consider another function of an unclear message, which is to disqualify itself by denying that anything is being said for which the speaker can be held responsible. Used in this way, unclear communication is a defensive device that enables a speaker to avoid responsibility for either himself/herself or for the message. Thus the metamessage becomes, "I am not really saying anything."

Chapter 3 discussed how all messages have the possibility of more than one meaning and the potential for being interpreted in various ways. Some families seem to adopt a chronic style of interacting that makes accurate interpretation especially difficult. This kind of self-disqualification of messages is easier to illustrate than to describe. It may include imcomplete sentences in which unfinished thoughts are left hanging in such a way that the listener is forced to make his own meaning ("What I really mean is . . . well, you know.") It may involve a kind of incoherence by interjection of meaningless phrases (again, "you know" is a current favorite), or by the overuse of nonquantifying qualifiers ("sort of," "kind of," "I mean," "that is") which add nothing to the meaning and tend to muddy the message. Indications of uncertainty ("I guess," "maybe," "I don't know") have the same effect when used excessively and also create a sense of extreme tentativeness. Loss of clarity may also occur because pronouns are used without clear referents, or when past-present switches make it difficult at best for the listener to know if the speaker is referring to a past or present situation, or speculating about the future.

Several varieties of unclear communication are to be found in the following illustration from Paul Watzlawick (1964), involving a discussion between a male patient and a therapist about the family's relationship to the husband's parents:

> *Therapist*: How does it work out, Mr. R_____, with your folks in town?
>
> *Husband:* Well we try, uh, very personally I mean . . . uh, I prefer that Jane takes the lead with them, rather than my taking the lead, oh . . . I like to see them, but I don't try too much to make it a point to be running over or have them . . . they know very definitely that . . . oh, it's always been even before Jane and I ever met and it was a thing that was pretty much just an accepted fact . . . in our family I was an only child . . . and they preferred that they would never, to the best of their ability, not, ah, interfere. I don't think there is . . . in any case I think there is always a . . . an underlying current there in my family, I don't care whether it's our family or any family. And it is something that even Jane and I feel when we . . . both of us are rather per-fectionists. And, ah . . . yet again, we're very . . . we are . . . st—rigid and uh . . . we expect that of the children but we feel that if you got to watch out, I mean, if, ah . . . you can have interference with in-laws, we feel, we've seen others with it we've just . . . it's been a thing that my own family tried to guard against, but ah, like here why we've . . . I wouldn't say we are stand-offish to the folks, but I prefer that the lead is always through Jane and its to her end (pp. 20–21).

As Watzlawick commented about this example, the thing that is particularly striking is this man's general incoherence. He seldom finishes a sentence, instead he leaves it up to the listener to supply the missing parts. His conversation contains an astonishing number of meaningless interjections, false starts, past-present switches, and personal pronouns whose referents are uncertain. Like other theorists, Watzlawick interprets these devices as "maneuvers in the service of defense against being held responsible or being put in the wrong by the other party" (p. 23).

Two empirical research studies of unclear family communication are relevant to this discussion. Morris & Wynne (1965) observed the communication habits of parents of schizophrenics and normals, and found in the parents of the schizophrenics a significantly higher incidence of drifting and scattered communication patterns, such as those just mentioned. Fisher, Boyd, Walker, & Shear (1959) compared the parents of twenty normal men, twenty neurotic men, and twenty schizophrenic men, using a battery of measures. The only measure that differentiated the parents was an interactional one derived from a joint Thematic Aperception Test (TAT) story. Parents of neurotics and normals were found to be significantly less ambiguous in their communication than were parents of schizophrenics. In discussing the significance of this finding, James Framo (1965) commented:

> It is likely, in this writer's judgment, that the *lack of clarity* of communication between parents and between each parent and the child is more pertinent to the development of the process type of schizophrenia in a child than is open disagreement and conflict; indeed, in some of the "sickest" families we have seen, there was very little open conflict. (pp. 429–430).

Incongruent Response

Incongruity can occur at a transactional level when the response is partially disjunctive with whatever went before, creating a discontinuity or break in the interaction. A response can also be incongruent because its verbal-nonverbal aspects do not seem to quite fit; that is, the message says something at a verbal level and denies it at a nonverbal level. Finally, a response is incongruent when its meaning is undecidable because it evokes a meaning at one logical level and denies that meaning at another level (creating paradox). Each of these forms of incongruity will be discussed in this section.

Transactional incongruity: The tangential response. We saw earlier in this chapter how a totally irrelevant response, often accompanied by monologue, is a severe enough disqualification to suggest indifference to the other and arouse in him the metamessage, "We are not communicating," and possibly the lethal metamessage, "You do not exist." In less extreme form, a response can create disjunction in the flow of interaction when it is only *partially* relevant to what has been said before, shifting or drifting to some other content. This form of communicative disjunction was first studied by Jurgen Ruesch (1958) as the "tangential response," one which occurs when a speaker reacts *selectively* to some incidental cue in another's utterance, but ignores or misses the primary point. Thus, the responder may acknowledge the other's attempt to communicate, but still rejects the other's theme or topic by shifting to another of his own. Ruesch noted that a speaker often picks up on a topic presented, but then continues to spin a yarn in a different direction (Speaking of that reminds me of . . . "). The response is not totally irrelevant because it has made some connection, although slight, with the prior utterance. Ruesch calls the tangential response "a selective reply, one that does not quite fit," and regards it as frustrating to the original speaker because it shifts to an aspect of the subject that is of no particular concern to him. Because such a response causes the first speaker to question the value or importance of whatever he/she was intending to relate, it is believed to adversely affect the speaker's sense of self-worth. It can also be guilt-arousing, particularly in the case of a tangential mother-child interaction sequence, as:

> *Child:* Mom, Joey hit me!
> *Mother:* Well, what did you do to make him hit you?
> or
> *Mother:* That's what you get for playing with those
> rough kids.

In either instance, the child was clearly making a bid for sympathy, and the response, although partially relevant to his complaint, did not cause the conversation to proceed in the way the child had intended.

The classic example of a tangential response is that of the small boy of five or so, who runs to his mother holding a worm and excitedly exclaims, "Mommy, look at the big fat worm I found!" She responds, "Go and wash your dirty hands!"

Regarding this example, Laing (1961) explained the disconfirming impact of the mother's response:

> In terms of the boy's feeling, the mother's response is at a
> tangent, as it were. She does not say, "Oh, yes, what a lovely
> worm." She does not say, "What a filthy worm—you musn't
> touch worms like that; throw it away." She does not express
> horror, approval, or disapproval of the *worm*, but she
> responds by focusing on something which he has not
> considered and which has no immediate importance to
> him, namely whether he is clean or dirty. (p. 86)

The tangential response is not, of course, limited to parent-
child interaction. In conversations between husband and wife,
a tangential response is often the means by which one or the
other takes the opportunity to file a cross-complaint, as in this
illustration:

> *Husband:* Eloise, why don't we ever have lamb any-
> more? I like lamb.
> *Wife:* So who can afford lamb on the paycheck you
> bring home?

Here Eloise's response sounds *almost* relevant, yet it is only
minimally connected to the subject of lamb, and merely opens
the door for a recurring battle about an entirely different
matter.

The tangential response is disconfirming because it les-
sens the worth of whatever the other person has said and
because it takes the conversation away from the speaker's
intended topic, cutting him/her off from whatever satisfaction
was anticipated from the conversation. Finally, the tangential
response can generate confusion in the mind of the initiator,
creating doubt as to what was really meant or wanted from the
conversation—an effect that can be especially damaging to a
child who is just beginning to master communication skills.

Transactional disqualification. The research team headed
by Carlos Sluzki (Sluzki, Beavin, Tarnopolski, & Veron, 1967)
labeled as "transactional disqualification" any incongruity in
the response of a speaker in relation to the context of the
previous message of the other (p. 494). They identified a

variety of near-irrelevances by studying family interaction sequences to determine how, and to what extent, each message related to whatever the prior speaker had just said. A relationship between successive messages exists, they decided, on two possible levels: (1) continuity between *contents* of the two messages (are both persons talking about the same subject?), and (2) indication of *reception* of the prior message (what cues does the responder give that he/she has received and understands the previous message?). If a message is disjunctive at either or both of these levels, transactional disqualification is said to have occurred.

According to Sluzki's analysis of this type of incongruity, if *a* is a statement that doesn't clearly end a topic of discussion, and *b*, the next utterance, is a new subject altogether, but contains no labeling of the switch (as, for example, "I'd like to bring up something else"), then *b* is disjunctive with regard to *a*. This represents discontinuity of content with no indication that the speaker has heard or acknowledged *a*, the prior message.

The following bit of interaction between mother and son in a family therapy session illustrates discontinuity at both levels:

> *a* Son: Well, then, I'll have to repeat again what I said. You, shall we say, started in this interview—of that I am sure—started to attack her first, that is, with nothing clarified, very hurried.
>
> *b* Mother: I love both of you, and I always try to make things at home work out better, but I can't manage it (Sluzki, et al., 1967, p. 469).

Another example of transactional disqualification is what Sluzki, et al., called the "sleight-of-hand" maneuver. This is a form of incongruity in which a change of subject is labeled as an answer to a preceding question. It implies that the responder has received the earlier message and is responding to it, when, in fact, does nothing of the sort. The response acknowledges receipt of the other's message, but violates content continuity. This sort of response occurs in many ordinary day-to-day situations, as when a speaker answers a question, "I'm glad you brought that up..." or "I've been meaning to talk with you about that," and then proceeds to talk about something quite different. Politicians, diplomats, and other public figures are generally expected to engage in sleight-of hand response as a way of evading undesired questions and befuddling their audience. Less simple to explain is the fact that mothers of schizophrenic children *also* tend to speak to their children in a similar manner. That is, they appear to be responding to whatever the child says, but actually have shifted to another topic (Beavers, et al., 1964, pp. 95–105).

A subtle form of the sleight-of-hand maneuver occurs when a responder makes a switch from the obvious content of the prior speech to a more literal level, but without labeling the switch as such. In the following example, a mother appears to be replying to her daughter's comment, but the response is not quite appropriate because the mother is using a word in a different sense from the daughter's use of the same word:

> *Daughter:* You treat me like a child.
> *Mother:* But you *are* my child.

In this illustration (Sluzki, et al. 1967), the daughter clearly meant that she was now grown up, not a small child any longer, while the mother refers to the daughter's biological status as her offspring. Significantly, the daughter is left without a rejoinder, and the point of her complaint is missed.

Verbal-Nonverbal incongruity. It goes without saying that meaning can be obscured when a speaker makes conflicting assertions—outright contradictions that occur when the speaker states a position and then denies the same position ("I'm really a happy person, only most of the time I feel sort of miserable"). It is equally evident that conflicting messages from two equally authoritative sources in the same family can create a sense of uncertainty in a child, as when one parent punishes and the other rewards the child for the same behavior. Such *contradictory* messages that confront each other directly seem less troublesome, however, then the message that denies itself in a different modality, as when a spoken message conflicts with its accompanying nonverbal metamessage from the same source.

As described in Chapter 2, meaning is made through various modalities: spoken words, voice qualities, facial expression, guestures, body position, and so on. These various modalities usually complement or reinforce each other and thus provide redundancy for any message (as when a mother says, "Come here," to a small child and holds out her arms). The two messages are incongruent with one another, however, if they evoke conflicting meanings in the listener. Thus, in the example just cited, the mother's verbal message and her extended arms would be congruent with each other, but incongruent with a harsh, cold, or threatening tone of voice.

When a loving verbal message is accompanied by a nonverbal message of rejection, the nonverbal message is considerably more believable, particularly to a small child. In this case, the speaker's tone of voice and body language carry more weight than do the spoken words, and this fact is of profound significance in understanding family pathology. As noted earlier, the wife who speaks seductive words but stiffens and withdraws from an intimate touch, or the mother who speaks to her child in loving words, but in an icy, threatening tone, are both familiar figures to a family therapist, as is the member who sends a verbal message but counteracts it with the nonverbal metamessage "this is play," or "don't take what I say seriously." In each of these instances the verbal messages are incongruent with their accompanying nonverbal messages, and the receiver must decide whether to believe the words or the other cues. A child may "resolve" the problem by trying to act on both verbal and nonverbal messages, or may simply withdraw from further interaction, finding the entire matter too threatening. Or the child may become skilled at sending incongruent messages of his/her own, since only incongruent communication makes sense in an incongruent system.

Logical incongruity and paradox. The notion of paradox,[*]

---

[*]This discussion of paradox draws heavily on Watzlawick, Beavin, & Jackson's *Pragmatics of Human Communication* (1967), especially their chapter 6 on "Paradoxical Communication," pp. 187–229.

once a plaything of philosophers and logicians, has in recent times become the serious concern of mathematicians and, still more recently, within the past few decades, has come to be a matter of interest in the fields of human interaction and human psychopathology. In 1956, with publication of the classic paper dealing with the double bind and schizophrenia (Bateson, et al., 1956) the subject of communicative paradox became accepted as significant in understanding the etiology of schizophrenia. In addition, paradox figures in Laing's concept of mystification and is a key factor in Wynne's pseudomutuality. It is included in this section because it represents a special sort of incongruity that is created by undecidable messages that say something at one logical level and deny it at another level.

Before attempting to explain the way in which logical incongruity between levels of meaning affects family psychopathology, we should take a brief look at the notion of paradox from its beginnings in antiquity.

The oldest known paradox dates back to early Greek times and has to do with the account of a man named Epimenides, a citizen of Crete, who reportedly said, "All Cretans are liars." The paradox is created because, if Epimenides was telling the truth, he was lying—and only if he was lying could he be telling the truth. This meets the requirements for a true paradox: *a logical contradiction following consistent deductions from correct premises.*

The account of Epimenides the Cretan is called a logico-mathematical paradox, a "solution" for which was advanced by Russell and Whitehead (1910) in their now-famous treatise on mathematics, *Principia Mathematica.* Their solution, known as the Theory of Logical Types, states that whatever involves *all* of a collection cannot itself be one of the collection. This is a logical safeguard that establishes that no totality may contain members that are definable only by means of the totality itself. The Theory of Logical Types resolved the problem of paradox for logicians, who were then able to point out that when Epimenides said that all Cretans are liars, he could not have been including himself in the collection "Cretan," therefore no paradox existed. However, solutions devised for mathematics and logic are often violated in human language behavior, so people have continued to send messages tantamount to "I am lying," and these assertions have continued to be undecidable to listeners because they contain both affirmation of a condition, and denial of that same condition at a different logical level.

As a theoretical solution to the logical paradox in language usage, Russell (1951) proposed what seems to be a corollary to the Theory of Logical Types in mathematics. Every language, he said, has a structure, concerning which nothing can be said—at least not in the same language. He suggested that *another* language would be needed to deal with the structure of the first language, and itself must have a new structure. According to this formulation (developed by Carnap in 1942 into a theory of levels of language) the lowest level of language can be indentified as *object* language. In order to say something about the object language, a meta-language must be employed. Viewed in this way, the statement of the lying Cretan can be seen as affirmation of a condition at the object level and denial of the same condition at the meta-language level. Applied to the speaker who says "I am lying," this theory also means that his assertion contains two distinct messages--one is on the object level and the other on the meta-level because it says something *about* the object-level message—namely, that it is untrue (Watzlawick, et al., 1967, p. 193). In the same way, the verbal injunction of a mother to her child ("Come to mother, darling") may be seen as an affirmation of her love on the object level, while simultaneously her tone of voice and bodily withdrawal are a denial of love at the meta-level ("I am lying"). As we saw earlier, a child is very aware of this kind of incongruity and seldom deceived.

In human interaction, participants can theoretically *step outside* the immediate content to talk about the communication itself (that is, to use the metacommunicative mode). However, as we have also seen before, powerful forces are often brought to bear on one who tries to do this, particularly if it is a child and the other person is the parent. If, in the example given, the child could comment on her mother's hostile tone ("Don't you like me, Mommy?"), the mother would doubtless deny that incongruity existed, with a reply like, "You must be imagining that, darling; you know how much Mother loves you." (Recall Laing's process of "mystification," in which a child's mode of experiencing is brought into question.) The matter might also inhibit the child's metacommunicative attempts by punishing her for her perceptiveness, as "You always get so upset over nothing!" Another way to inhibit the child's attempt to metacommunicate might be simply to appear unable to see the point of her comment or to make any sense of it—a devastating form of disqualification. In either case, a child who attempts to confront a parent at the metacommunicative level is usually caught in a trap, as Bateson, et al. (1956) noted:

> The only way the child can really escape from the situation is to comment on the contradictory position his mother has put him in. However, if he did so, the mother would take this as an accusation that she is unloving and both punish him and insist that his perception of the situation is distorted. By preventing the child from talking about the situation, the mother forbids him using the metacommunicative level—the level we use to correct our perception of communicative behavior. (p. 357)

This sort of inhibition of a "victim" from commenting about an incongruity when confronted with conflicting messages is of some consequence in family interaction. The solution to the dilemma is for the person to inquire, "What do you really mean?" Then he or she can step outside the object language, thus destroying the paradox.

The *paradoxical injunction* is a special kind of paradox that involves the giving of an order that connot be obeyed without *dis*obeying it. In its most common form, one person tells another to do something while, at another logical level, ensures that he *cannot* do it. This differs from a simple contradiction in that the order contains its own negation. If, for instance, a driver were confronted at an intersection with a traffic light showing both red and green at the same time, the situation would present a contradiction and the driver would simply have to decide (guess?) which of the two conflicting instructions to follow, knowing that one choice would be right.

However, if the driver passed a roadside sign that read, "Ignore this sign," this would be a true paradoxical injunction, for by obeying the sign, the driver could *not* obey it. Paradoxes involve differences in *levels* of meaning and should not be confused with simple inconsistences or contradictions, as Haley (1967) noted:

> If a man says, "I won't stand for that any more!" in a tone of voice which indicates anger and with a gesture of putting a stop to it in a situation where what he says is appropriate, then his statement and disqualifications can be said to be congruent, or to "affirm" each other. Messages and their qualifiers can also be incongruent. If a mother makes a punishing staement while labeling what she says as benevolent, she is... manifesting an incongruence between her levels of message. It is important to note that she is not contradicting herself. Contradictory statements are of the same level: "I will do it," and "I won't do it." Incongruent statements are of different levels: "I will do it," said in a tone of voice which indicates "Don't take what I say seriously." (p. 258)

The distinction between paradox and contradiction is important in understanding some psychopathologies. Simple contradictions can be demonstrated in experimental conditions in which approach-avoidance conflict is induced in animals. In such experiments, the animal subject may experience anxiety because it must make decisions involving some risk to itself, but serious pathology seldom is observed as a result. Paradox is illustrated by the Pavlovian-type experiments in which a dog is trained to discriminate between a circle (associated with punishment) and an ellipse (associated with reward), following which the ellipse is gradually expanded to appear more and more like a circle. In this way, experimental neurosis is induced in the animal as the ellipse begins to contain *within itself* an element of the feared circle, and there is no choice the animal can make to resolve the paradox except to withdraw from the whole distressing situation. It has been surmissed that a child who is regularly faced with situations in which he or she cannot obey a parental injunction at one level without disobeying it at another might behave in a similar fashion—with anxiety, neurosis, or psychotic withdrawal from reality.

The *double bind* is a pathological form of parodoxical injunction that has been noted in families with a schizophrenic member (Bateson, et al., 1956). The double-bind hypothesis of schizophrenia holds that the mother of a schizophrenic child, in her verbal and nonverbal interaction with him, presents messages that are mutually incompatible at different logical levels (the object level and the meta-level). As a consequence the child is continually placed in a situation where she/he can't win. Like the dog faced with a slightly flattened circle, the child receives messages to which he is afraid to respond, and at the same time is afraid *not* to respond, because they contain their own negation and are therefore undecidable. The prototype of this kind of double message is the injunction, "Be spontaneous!" which cannot be obeyed without following an order—which, of course, destroys the spontaneity. Similar examples can be found in the father who orders his son not to defy him; yet he also complains that his son doesn't stand up to him like a man; or the mother who tells her daughter to be "a little lady," yet the first gift she sends her at a girl's detention home is a set of seven sexy, different-colored brassieres (Satir, 1967, p. 37). Although seemingly trivial as a causative factor in serious pathology, this kind of incongruent message-sending, when habitual, has been cited as a correlate of both schizophrenia and various personality disorders. Cameron (1963) commented:

> In actual cases studied, the more significant parent—usually but not always the mother—has been observed encouraging amoral or antisocial behavior in the child without consciously realizing it ... In some cases reported, a parent showed unmistakable relish while the child was telling the therapist about his misdeeds, as though the recital were pleasureably wicked, but once the tale was told the parent turned immediately moralistic and condemned it and the child. (p. 654)

According to the original form of the double-bind hypothesis, five ingredients are necessary for a family situation to become double-binding:

(1) Two or more person, one being the "victim."

(2) Repeated experience, so that the double bind becomes a recurring theme in the victim's experience.

(3) A primary negative injunction ("If you do not do so-and-so, I will punish you," or "Do not do so-and-so, or I will punish you.")

(4) A secondary injunction, of a different logical order, conflicting with the first and, like the first, enforceable by punishment.

(5) A third injunction prohibiting the victim from leaving the field.

Finally, of course, the complete set of requirements is no longer necessary when the victim has learned to perceive his or her universe in a double-bind pattern (Bateson, et al., 1956, p. 253).

As originally conceived, the double-bind hypothesis applied only to dyadic relationships between mother and schizophrenic child. Later Weakland (1960) extended application of the hypothesis to three-party interaction; and Ferreira (1960) studied the mother-father-child triad in non-schizophrenic families, concluding that double-binds have a universality much greater than schizophrenia. It is apparent, too, that adult-to-adult communication can also be double-binding, although the adult generally has more loopholes for escape.

Despite the fact that most published examples of the double-bind involve interaction in which one person appears to be "binding" the other, it is important to note that people frequently put each other in mutually untenable positions, as Laing (1961) commented:

> One must remember that the child may put his parents into untenable positions. The baby cannot be satisfied. It cries "for" the breast. It cries when the breast is presented. It cries when the breast is withdrawn. Unable to "click with" or "get through," mother becomes intensely anxious and feels hopeless. She withdraws from the baby in one sense, and becomes over-solicitous in another sense. Double binds can be two-way. (pp. 128–129)

CONFIRMING RESPONSE

Thus far in this chapter we have looked at disconfirming kinds of response, especially as they occur in family interaction. It is now time to consider confirming styles of response—those behaviors that evoke in the receiver feelings of being *recognized, acknowledged,* and *endorsed.* These feelings can also be described in terms of behaviors believed to evoke the feeling of confirmation in others. Each of these groups of behaviors provides limited confirmation, but only when all three elements are evident in a particular communicative relationship can a person experience his or her own being and significance, as well as connectedness with others in a way that acknowledges his/her "otherness."

Recognition

Recognition of another evokes the metamessages, "I am aware of your presence" and "I am willing to relate to you." Behaviorally, recognition is expressed in ways that are both nonverbal and verbal: looking at the other, paying attention to him/her without attending to other matters, making frequent eye contact, responding with appropriate facial expression or vocalization, and touching. Verbally, recognition means responding relevantly, using personal language and authentic self-expression, allowing the other the opportunity to also respond, eschewing monologue in favor of reciprocal exchange. In short, it means treating others with respect, being aware of their existence, their attempts to make contact, to relate, and to have a presence in the world.

Acknowledgment

Acknowledgment evokes the dual metamessages, "You are a unique human being of worth and significance," and "We are communicating." It serves the function of furthering, facilitating, and encouraging continued communication and, at the same time, enables the speaker to feel understood and appreciated. Acknowledging response is transactionally congruent in that it directly (not tangentially) follows what the other has said. This does not require praise or even agreement, but simple conjunction with the other's communication. Buber recognized this when he wrote that mutually confirming partners can still "struggle together in direct opposition" (Friedman, 1960), and Laing (1961) made a similar point, saying that even rejection can be confirming if it is direct, not tangential, and if it grants significance and validity to what the other says (p. 82). Acknowledgment also means that response is clear, direct, and unambiguous; its verbal aspects are congruent with the accompanying nonverbal behavior, as well as congruent at the logical level; that is, both object-level messages and meta-level messages are in agreement.

Endorsement

Endorsement evokes the metamessage, "I accept your perceptions as valid." Behaviorally, it expresses acceptance of the other person and his/her feelings as they are described, by simply letting them be, without blame, analysis, justification, modification, or denial. It means allowing the other to speak for himself/herself, act automomously, and take self-responsibility.

CHAPTER 14

Toward Synthesis: Four Family Systems

A family is a field for forces; no single aspect can be studied or fully understood apart from the total field. Communication is inextricably woven into the fabric of the family's life together: its communication cannot be separated from its systems characteristics, its internal and external relational patterns, its potential pathologies, or its members' habitual forms of response to one another.

Communication in a family serves and supports the character of its system and its existing relationships. Any major change in a family's interactional style sets into motion relational changes and whole-system changes. It is for this reason that family therapy is often successful; the therapeutic creation of disequilibrium in the system can influence and change individual functioning—and individual change brings about change in the structure of the total system.